Endorsements

This beautiful book is a gift that you can give to yourself or loved ones. This work of art will hold your dreams while you are creating them and long after they come true.

—Marcia Wieder, Founder & CEO, Dream University

I've had the good fortune of being able to speak all over the world, working with great men like Jim Rohn, Zig Ziglar, and Les Brown. I've developed a passion for personal development, and I've learned that the ability to dream is paramount to success. Unfortunately, many have lost their ability to dream. *My Dream Book* takes you on a step-by-step journey that will teach you how to dream again and how to take action on those dreams. You can dream again! *My Dream Book* will make that easier!

—Gary Eby, Author, International Trainer, and Sales Strategist

My Dream Book entices me to sit down and write. I love that I have space to add my own pictures. Some dreams actually do come true! I am sure a lot of people will enjoy using *My Dream Book.*

—Maria Neubauer, ISF Internationale Schule, Frankfurt-Rhein-Main, Germany

My Dream Book

Tom & Kathy,

May all your dreams come true!

Lisa Boyd Wykes

Lisa Boyd

My Dream Book

Journal To Discover Your Destiny

Tate Publishing & *Enterprises*

Dedication

I would like to dedicate this book to my family, beginning with my mom, Marge, who always had high aspirations. Being a dreamer herself, she taught me how to dream as a little girl. Thanks for never letting on for one moment as if those dreams might not come true. You laid an amazing spiritual foundation in my life, which led me to where I am today. You always told me we'd be rich one day, and compared to our humble beginnings, I would say we are, Mom.

To my beautiful sister, Janice, her grown children, Mashelle, Chad, and their families, all dreamers themselves; I am so grateful for your optimism and your willingness for risk-taking to have the abundant life our Lord came to give. Mashelle, my niece, my childhood playmate and business partner, there are no words that can express my appreciation for your deep understanding, vision, and enthusiasm for *My Dream Book*. And likewise, Janice, for your friendship, support, amazing words of encouragement, and for the faith and confidence you build in me with your heartfelt compliments, I remain speechless.

Julia and Mikaela, my beautiful angels, thank you for telling me countless times that I am *the greatest mother ever* (a title I feel most unworthy to hold). Markus and Lukas, *I didn't know you were going to be here!* God performed a miracle the day he brought you two into my life. Thank you for the life lessons and the laughs, especially during the hard times. Because of you four in my life, I have been blessed tremendously. You are proof that dreams come true.

To the memory of my best and late friend, Kathy Muse; you were like a sister to me, unconditionally loving, always believing in me. I know that you are looking down from the heavens, rejoicing for the things God has done. There have been many tomorrows that were hard to face without you, but as you always signed your letters, "Because He Lives."

Dick and Pat Hennings, you did the unthinkable by opening your heart and home to me during my lost and confusing teenage years. Thank you for the tremendous musical foundation, leadership, and support through the FBC Youth Ministry. Brother "Duck," you made an impact in all our young lives that will never be forgotten. Thank you, Pat, for all the confidence-boosting, long talks, lectures, prayers, and tears. You will always be my hero.

Kurt, thank you for the many lessons learned and especially for supporting my MLM product gambles. I was terrible at them, but through those failed business ventures, I found something more valuable, something I'd lost along the way—my ability to dream. It was through motivational speakers the company suggested that I was challenged where and when I needed it the most.

Jonathan, we've been through a lot, you and I. Eons ago you suggested cutting magazine pictures to make something called a "dream book." We never finished, but I kept our clippings to complete it someday. Finally that *someday* is here. Thank you for introducing me to the concept and for being a dreamer at heart.

To all the dreamers out there: may you follow the model of Joseph, also known as the *Prince of Egypt*. Though you may find yourself in the dungeon, expect that a miracle may happen at any moment to make your dreams come true.

And last, but certainly not least, I would like to thank my husband, Michael, for being my daily life support, and the provider who has made my dream not only possible, but a reality. Your sacrifice, suggestions, and patience have been greatly appreciated. I love you.

No one's ever seen or heard anything like this. Never so much as imagined anything quite like it- What God has arranged for those who love him.

1 Corinthians 2:9 (MSG)

But as it is written: Eye has not seen, nor ear heard, nor have entered into the heart of man the things which God has prepared for those who love Him.

1 Corinthians 2:9 (NKJV)

Table of Contents

Foreword

Lisa is one of the few people I have encountered on this path of life who is truly a free spirit. Most of us get bogged down in the demands and responsibilities of daily life and lose that part of ourselves. But Lisa uses her experiences from daily life as a stimulus to let her free spirit play and create. This book is evidence of this creative play as one begins to let ones free spirit wander down life's road, seeking our own dreams. Some people are the caretakers of wonder. Lisa is one of these people, and her book helps us get in touch with this wonder. As we explore our dreams both little and big, we begin to choose the dream that makes our hearts sing. She then gives us hope that we can pursue that dream and make it come alive. This book truly inspires the directionless soul onto a path of self-discovery as a dreamseeker.

—Marleen Weaver
M.A., M.S., L.P.C.

Section 1:

The Assessment

"Keep your heart open to dreams. For as long as there's a dream, there is hope, and as long as there is hope, there is joy in living."

—Anonymous

Finally there is a book to create what many have referred to over the years as a "dream book." I became frustrated when trying to find one to purchase for a graduation gift. I'd always wanted to make one for myself, but all that I ended up with was a file of magazine clippings and a cheap spiral with some notes. While I wrote my dreams in that spiral, it still didn't really feel like my *dream book*. This is the book I tried to find. It is a journal for recording your lifelong dreams. Some will be grand, and some may seem insignificant. The fulfillment of seemingly small dreams sometimes brings great joy, so don't overlook them. Take each section seriously, as you will learn much about yourself if you do.

Having some basic ideas of what you want in life, you may still fall into one of several categories.

- One, you're rather clueless; you know very little about yourself and what you want out of life. You drift along in survival mode most days and hope for the best. You know you want more, but you have been unaware of your power to take control and create something more significant.

- Two, you know what you would like, but you've lost all hope that you'll ever have it. You don't expect miraculous things to happen anymore.

- Three, your life is pretty good, and you think of yourself as a happy person. You're not really in touch with your dreams, though, and you have not lived up to your potential. You've yet to tap into the creative genius that I believe exists in all people.

- Four, you know yourself and what you want. You need an organized place to record your dreams and want to pursue them. You are ready to utilize the tools offered in this book to design your destiny and live the life of your dreams.

No matter what category you fall into, this book is for you. Everyone has dreams and deserves the opportunity to explore them. In *Oh, the Places You'll Go*, Dr. Seuss has a few things to say about living the life of your dreams. One of the opening statements in this book is: "You have brains in your head. You have feet in your shoes. You can steer yourself any direction you choose."

It is easy to lose sight of your aspirations. You can become so accustomed to feelings of chronic boredom that they become a part of your identity. You may hold on to these feelings and even defend having them. This can happen with you completely unaware of what is taking place within. There's actually an "emotional payoff," when one feels like a victim of his or her life. It is easy to get stuck there and feel comfortable with it in a weird, unhealthy way. Negative emotions are actually addictive. Think about all the sad songs and how popular they are. Most of us love a good pity party, especially when it's thrown in our honor and we take the opportunity to indulge in "poor me" feelings. Challenge yourself to take a hard look at where you are and what changes you may need to make in this area.

As much as anything else, this book is about change. It is about getting out of a rut you're stuck in because I believe that you can change. You can change your life, and you can change your world starting today. This self-revolution will require determination and a commitment to certain daily practices. Ultimately you will need a plan for yourself. The pursuit of the empowering knowledge necessary to make a paradigm shift in your automatic thinking will, of course, be a daily one. A life-changing transformation will take place as you *change the way you think, both consciously and subconsciously.* This book can help you experience the marvelous changes that personal development can bring, enabling you to share your dreams and journey with others.

You may feel frustrated in the beginning, but eventually you'll understand that even more important than the end result is the journey you take to arrive there. Ben Sweetland taught that success is a journey, not a destination. I believe the journey begins the minute you change your mind and decide to go for your dreams. Choosing to feel hopeful and powerful instead of hopeless and pitiful will impact your life starting today.

Be prepared for distractions along the way and realize that recommitting yourself to the journey each day is one of the secrets to success. Utilizing this book will help you stay on track. Also, my company's Web site: http://www.one-stop-dream-shop.com will be a great resource for completing your dream book.

Hoping and believing in your dreams is energizing, bringing to life the magic you once experienced in childhood. Many ignore their dreams, even small ones, in spite of the endless hours spent daydreaming. Few will do anything about their dreams except tuck them away in their hearts to quietly die. But it doesn't have to be that way!

Decide to start your journey toward success today and use this journal as your starting block on the track of success. Making use of simple but powerful concepts, you will find user-friendly, detailed instructions in *My Dream Book.* If you do not know where to start with a certain subject, again you can visit my Web site for ideas. My company is continually updating our site with valuable information on the subject of making your dreams come true. Even subjects like your dream style or your dream furnishings are explored.

In *My Dream Book,* you will explore who you are, regardless of your age or predicament, and use this self-discovery guide to get in touch with your heart's desires. Eventually, you will create a plan to reach your goals. Don't be afraid to just start writing, as you are allowed to cross out and make revisions along the way. It won't be hard either; it will be fun. As the creative process within you begins, you will find your thoughts beginning to flow naturally.

Knowing who you are and living life with a focused purpose may be a new experience. Most likely, you'll find you do it in some areas already. Discovering how to express yourself through living the life you were meant to live is your contribution to the earth; we just may need what you have to offer. You are, after all, the only *you* this world will ever know, and this is your time if you dare to take it. Have the courage to try something new, take a few risks, and really live!

My Dream Book is a place for discovering your desires, listing your interests, and organizing your goals. Today may be the day you start your life makeover. Life makeovers begin when you start changing the way you think. Change the way you think, and you will change your life.

My belief in the power of our dreams came from my own experiences reading sacred texts like the Bible, studying personal development materials created by successful people and from researching numerous sources on the Internet. Of course, it didn't happen overnight. As I've heard it said, "I haven't arrived yet, but I sure have left!" Remarkably, my thought life has radically improved over the last several years.

My Journey

Having had a tragic childhood, I naturally created a tragic adulthood. I once was very discouraged with what seemed like a life of failures. In spite of the success I did experience, I truly thought and felt like a loser. Somehow, though, I couldn't stop hoping for a better way of life. I started becoming more and more honest with myself and confronting my negative thinking.

I still remember the day when it hit me hard that I did not expect real success would ever be mine. I observed myself thinking and feeling resigned to this, and I was shocked. All of my life people had told me I was beautiful, talented, and smart, yet I realized that I didn't even feel worthy to experience one moment of real success. I knew then I had to make a change. If I didn't expect anything good to ever happen to me, how in the world could it?

I became a seeker, and an avid reader. I read books like *Think and Grow Rich* by Napoleon Hill, *Grow Rich While You Sleep* by Ben Sweetland, and *The Power of Your Subconscious Mind* by Dr. Joseph Murphy. During this time, I came upon a concept that was new to me. Books like *Dare to Win* by Jack Canfield and Mark Victor Hansen, and *The Secret* by Rhonda Byrne teach that the power to realize our dreams is within each of us using the "Law of Attraction." In *The Master Key System* by Charles F. Haanel, he defines the Law of Attraction as the idea that "thought is a creative energy, and will automatically correlate with its object and bring it into manifestation." Whether this is an actual *law* or not, certainly there seems to be much truth in the teaching that what we dwell upon will affect how we feel, what we do, and ultimately what we receive.

The same teaching is actually all throughout the Old and New Testaments. It's really nothing new, but it is being perceived in a new light and perhaps with a different focus. The late author and minister Dr. Joseph Murphy, whom I mentioned earlier, taught that we were born to be rich, prosperous, and to live an abundant life. The following is a summary of his central teaching regarding our life purpose and is good food for thought:

You grow rich by the use of your God-given faculties, by tuning in with the Infinite, and as your mind becomes…productive and full of good ideas, your labor will become more productive and will bring you all kinds of…material riches…There is no virtue whatsoever in poverty, which in actual fact is a mental disease, and it should be abolished from the face of the earth. You are here to find your true place in life, and to give of your talents to the world…You are here to expand and unfold in a wonderful way, according to a God-given potential, and to bring forth spiritual, mental, and material riches, which will bless humanity in countless ways.

If you have felt inferior or insignificant most of your life, imagine the potentially positive changes that can occur when embracing these beliefs about yourself. If instead of focusing on your limitations, you focused on your creative potential, imagine the impact this could have on your world. If, as the Butterfly Effect suggests, a butterfly flapping its wings here ultimately influences the weather on the other side of the world, surely a ripple of joy could have grand effects across our planet.

Many leaders in personal development embrace the belief that your subconscious mind and your internal dialogue greatly influence and set the course for your life. Goal writing, visualizing, and using declarative and positively affirming statements are all tools that can help you change your thinking and build your faith for a better tomorrow. Changing ones perspective has been proven over and over to change lives. Perhaps there are things you would like to change about yours?

The power to influence and change your life is not really in the hands of those around you but within you. I believe you have the opportunity and responsibility to live a full, purposeful existence and that it is your birthright. You owe it to yourself and those around you. Give yourself an opportunity by committing to use this book. Take its suggestions and give your dreams a chance. I think you'll find you've nothing to lose and a better lifestyle to gain.

Write your dreams in this book enthusiastically, just as if putting them here will make them come true. While using this book, allow yourself to use your imagination. Feel a sense of excitement, as if your dreams were truly on order to come true! You can brainstorm, read, search the Internet, go shopping, and visit used bookstores for purchasing magazines or travel books. Eventually, I see you sitting down with your *Dream Book*, your magazines, laptop, or favorite beverage, and beginning to dream.

> "So … be your name Buxbaum or Bixby or Bray or Mordecai Ali
> Van Allen O'Shea, you're off to Great Places! Today is your day!
> Your mountain is waiting. So … get on your way!"
> —Dr. Seuss, from *Oh, the Places You'll Go*

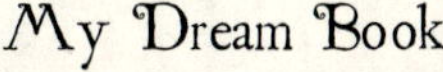

Taking Your Personal Inventory

The reason most people never reach their goals is that they don't define them, learn about them, or ever seriously consider them as believable or achievable. Winners can tell you where they are going, what they plan to do along the way, and who will be sharing the adventure with them.

—Denis Waitley

Below is a brief outline or plan for creating the life of your dreams.

- Explore your dreams

- Discover your hidden desires and talents

- Clarify your dreams

- Develop an awareness of any limiting beliefs you may hold

- Challenge the obstacles standing in the way of reaching your goals

- Visualize the success your dreams deserve

- See them come to realization and completion

On the following pages you will begin your personal inventory and take your first steps toward knowing who you are, where you want to go, and how you are going to arrive there.

> Manifesting your goals and life dreams does not depend on your education or on your ethnicity or cultural heritage and is in no way determined by your environment. It is only the result of how and what you think!
> —Thomas Herold, **Founder & CEO of Dream Manifesto**

Name ten things about your current job, career, or education that leave you feeling disappointed or bored:

I ____

____

____

____

2 ____

____

____

____

3 ____

____

____

____

Personal Inventory

4

5

6

7

8

9 ____

____

____

10 ____

____

____

____

Name ten things about your current home, including décor and furniture, that invoke feelings of disappointment or boredom:

1 ____

____

____

____

2 ____

____

____

____

3 ____

____

Personal Inventory

4

5

6

7

8

9 _______________________________

____

____

____

10 _______________________________

____

____

____

Name ten things about your current friendships, family ties, or romantic relationship that find you feeling angry, confused, disappointed, hurt, or bored:

1 _______________________________

____

____

____

2 _______________________________

____

____

____

Personal Inventory

3

4

5

6

7

8 ____

____

____

____

____

9 ____

____

____

____

10 ____

____

____

____

Personal Inventory

Look at the negative statements you wrote on the previous pages. Pick all or some of the statements and change the wording so that it becomes an "I want" statement. For example, "My ugly bedroom furniture doesn't match" becomes "I want to have a beautiful, color-coordinated, matching bedroom set."

1 ____

____

____

____

2 ____

____

____

____

3 ____

____

____

____

4 ____

____

____

5 ____

____

____

____

6 ____

____

____

____

7 ____

____

____

____

____

8 ____

____

____

____

9 ____

____

____

Personal Inventory

Read over the lists that you have made and note the areas of your life in which you want to make improvements. Begin imagining these areas becoming the way you want, and trust that the process has begun. As you begin filling in different sections of the book, use these lists as references while identifying your specific dreams. Elaborate more in the individual sections as you begin formulating your dreams.

Getting started

when you dont Know where to start

If looking through this book results in you feeling overwhelmed, go to your calendar and schedule a day to do the following activity:

- Find magazines of all types and begin flipping pages (a used book store is a great place). Clip any images, words, or stories that appeal to you. It doesn't matter if you don't understand why something attracts you. Just have fun!

- When you are done, spread out your clippings and begin browsing

- Take a piece of paper and start jotting down a short description or title for each picture. See any similar themes?

- You could create a graphic organizer like a word web by drawing a big circle in the middle (see the Web site address below for examples). Put your name or a category in the center and draw lines to other circles. Begin writing descriptions of the images in each circle. As you complete the exercise, notice without judgment your tastes, desires, and interests. An excellent

resource for finding a selection from which to choose
and print these graphic organizers is http://www.edu-
place.com/graphicorganizer/

Perhaps look over the table of contents and make plans to explore each subject by reading, brainstorming, researching, and dreaming about those areas of your life. Eventually, what interests or excites you will be turned into goals. Try to be as detailed as possible when completing the pages in *My Dream Book*. At first it will be more important to start brainstorming than to actually pinpoint your answers. You may only write a word or two, but you will be adding more information as your visions for your future become clearer.

Getting Started

Using Affirmations

to Visualize Your Goals and Encourage Your Spirit

So What Is an Affirmation Anyway?

Though I'd heard and read about people having success with affirmations, the word did not really have a tangible meaning for me. Eventually I explored some definitions that were helpful. The term *positive confession* is used similarly, and I think of these as *faith-thoughts* that can be used either with your inner voice or spoken aloud. At any rate, these affirmative statements can be very powerful tools in changing your life for the better. It is imperative for you to be open to the idea that you really can be blessed with what you truly desire. I don't mean to imply magic here but simply suggest we often do receive what we ask for when we ask in faith and with good intentions. The biggest problem is that we often forget to ask. So deciding it is okay to ask for what we want may be the place to start.

Many people reflect at some point in their lives having realized they felt less worthy and less deserving than other people. I have found affirmations tremendously helpful. The hardest part of using them is getting organized, so I have included pages in this book for you to write them down.

For starters, here are some descriptions that may be helpful:

- An admission that something, which may not yet be visible or verifiable, is true.

- An absolute judgment.

- A statement affirming the existence of the truth of something hoped for.

- A disciplined application in focusing your intentions and creating prayers to get results based on the conviction that your faith-thoughts and prayers create your destiny.

- Positive declarations used with as much feeling as one can muster, thus backing the affirmation with feeling, which gives it more power to bloom.

When using affirmations, it is important to write your dreams as if you have already achieved them. It will feel strange at first. Believe me, I know. When I wrote "I am a published author" in mine two years ago, I felt a little silly and had no idea what I would even write about. But if you are holding this book, then you know that my dream came true. So dare to be a little silly. It is a *dream book*, after all!

A technique that works very effectively is to make bold "I" statements in the present tense. For example, "I choose to eat healthy foods and exercise on a regular basis." Then act and feel as if that is the reality in your life right now. Do this so that you can experience how it would feel to have achieved your dream, thus opening your mind up to unlimited possibilities. This is an important step toward

Using Affirmations

your success for so many reasons. Remember, your mind, hand in hand with your faith, can move mountains!

> My word be that goes forth from my mouth; It shall not return to Me void; But it shall accomplish what I please, and it shall prosper in the thing for which I sent it.
>
> Isaiah 55:10–11, NKJV

> The Divine Spirit that gives me my dreams leads me through my intuitions, and shows me at the perfect time, the path to take to success.

Using the above affirmation as an example, write your own affirmations or faith declarations about seeing your dreams fulfilled.

____

____

____

____

Revisit and Re-write Your Goals Often

People who write their goals down and review them regularly have been proven to have a higher rate of achievement. Writing down our goals, both large and small, is crucial to seeing them accomplished. Dr. Gail Matthews, a psychology professor associated with the Dominican University of California, conducted a study concluding that people who write their goals down and share them with someone trusted, with whom they communicate weekly, were _at least_ 33 percent more successful in reaching their goals than those who did not. It's not the only formula for success, but it does strongly indicate that the chances of reaching your goals can be greatly improved.

Motivational speaker Zig Ziglar recommends you "invest ten minutes a day in reviewing your goals and ambitions. Think about what you want and how far you (will go) have gone to reach it … by doing this, your mind will start to focus on transforming them into a strategy and then, through action, into reality."

Review your dream book each night before bedtime, first thing in the morning, or both. Set your course so that you know where you are going in each area of your life versus ending up whichever way the wind blows that day.

Create Visual Aids to Stimulate Your Subconscious Mind

Never underestimate how powerful *vision page* exercises can be to bring about the change you want. Paste or use scrapbooking tape to place pictures on the designated *vision* pages throughout your dream book. Create a collage to put on your bulletin board. For example, if your dream is to write, then surround your office with books about your area of interest and pictures or magazine clippings that support the writer's mentality and reinforce your dream in your subconscious mind. The mirror is an excellent place for affirmations. To do this attractively, take your affirmations to a print shop and have them copied onto transparent sheets. You will see them first thing in the morning and right before you go to bed. Choose a private place, like the back of your closet door, if you prefer to keep your dreams secret for now.

Visualization

Visualization is a powerful tool to rewrite the original programming of your subconscious mind. This process opens your conscious mind up to allow new beliefs of success, hope, and contentment into your powerful subconscious mind. Here are some exercises you can do anytime, anywhere:

- Visualize checking your bank balance and finding a large sum of money.

 Using Affirmations

- Imagine feeling really successful and recognized in your career.

- Picture your life changing quickly, simply, and easily.

- If you need a new car, daydream that you are sitting behind the wheel; feel the leather interior and experience the new car smell.

- Feel the happiness of a fulfilling relationship.

Begin with simple activities like these every day before you even get out of bed or as you fall asleep each night. These experiences will help your mind open up to the possibility of expecting what you truly desire.

I Am Thankful For…

Take time to make a gratitude list each day. A common teaching among those featured in *The Secret* by Byrne is to make a grateful attitude of major importance in your daily life. Thinking about this led me to thoughts of the difference between "I wish" statements made in a negative complaining spirit and "I Wish" statements made from hopeful, productive dreaming. True dreaming begins in a space of gratefulness. You see the abundance already present in your life, and you feel grateful. Seeing yourself as blessed, you, therefore, are confident to ask for more blessings, and in this process you will become a blessing to others. Being grateful actually builds your faith!

Some days it may only be that you are alive, in good health, or have a roof over your head. Sometimes you may find yourself wanting to complain, but remember, some people literally live on the streets. Fighting self-pity is a biggie and will keep you stuck where you are. If you find you are feeling sorry for yourself in some area of your life, think about the basic luxuries you have like a car, a bed, or food to eat. Find any opportunity you can to be grateful. When you feel thankful, your energy changes, and you will feel and think differently.

It is truly transforming to make thoughts of gratitude your first thought of the day. You will feel happier if you make a concerted effort to feel grateful every day of your life for something. If you notice negative thoughts about yourself creeping in, visit our Web site. Read inspirational stories or visit the affirmations page to commit one to memory. Go to your journal and begin to write declarative faith statements.

In support of my position on the power of our words, I offer what I heard from Joel Osteen on television one morning. He is the author of *Your Best Life Now* and *The Power of Words*.

> Your words have creative power. Your words can build up or tear down. Your words can bring victory or defeat. Your words affect your future. You can speak life and encouragement or strife and division. When you speak God's Word over your life, you set into motion the very thing you declare.

I think of this in terms of the written word, as well as the words we speak. The ultimate goal is to change the words we speak over our lives on a daily basis. Take control of life instead of letting life control you. Empower yourself using the activities, suggestions, and information offered in this book to create the life of your dreams.

When you feel grateful, your daydreaming no longer comes from a victim's mentality. On the contrary, it will spring forth from a believer's mentality—a way of thinking that believes God resides in a place of rich abundance. A mentality that recognizes a presence pleased to bless from that endowment. You will know there is no lack, so there is no fear in dreaming. Dreaming then becomes a faith-filled activity as you imagine the good things you desire easily manifesting in your life, blessing you and others richly.

> Gratitude is a powerful process for shifting your energy and bringing more of what you want into your life. Be grateful for what you already have, and you will attract more good things.
> from *The Secret* by Rhonda Byrne

Using Affirmations

On the lines below, list the things in your life for which you can feel grateful today.

____

____

____

____

____

____

____

____

____

____

____

____

The "I Wish..." Worksheet

Embrace this God-life. Really embrace it, and nothing will be too much for you. This mountain, for instance: Just say, Go jump in the lake—no shuffling or shilly-shallying—and it's as good as done. That's why I urge you to pray for absolutely everything, ranging from small to large. Include everything as you embrace this God-life, and you'll get God's everything.

Mark 11:24–25 (The Message Bible)

My Wish List

So, in order to change, I can write a list: "I want..." I may write down 20 things or 120. I don't analyze or criticize anything... This doesn't mean I'm going to get everything I want. However, if I learn what I want, then I can learn to ask.

—Kurt-Edouard Neubauer

Abandoning all reservations, begin writing sentences that begin with *I Wish,* letting the sentences flow from your hand instead of deliberating over what you want. Purpose to write what you *do* want. If there are areas of your life where you don't know what you want but know what you don't, then include them. Try and find the most positive way to write these sentences in order to avoid this becoming just a complaining session or opportunity to feel sorry for yourself.

My Purpose

Live Laugh Love *Be Still* And Know *Grow* See Smile Learn To Love *Find Inner Peace* **Find Love** Live An Adventure Find *Enlightenment* Inspire **Express** Redefine Envision *Empower Others* Motivate *Shine* **Be Blessed** And Bless Others Enjoy Oneself Be Challenged Give Joyfully Express Teach Pursue **Smile** Advise Live Experience Explore *Envision* Inspire **Mystify** Enchant Devise Minister *Awaken* Guide Sing See *Pray* Explain **Invent** Unify Bless Model *Accept Myself* And *Others* See *Beauty* **Improve** Enhance Produce Exhort Connect Counsel Govern *Love Build* Relationship **Predict** *Help* Share Gain Knowledge *Spread* Know Launch Beautify Create Peace **Investigate** Flow Be One Serve Heal *Be Faithful* Systematize Play Dance **Increase** Draw Illustrate *Color* Portray Lead Research Invent See *Design* Live **Laugh** Love All Be One Enrage Justify *Enlighten* Inspire Encourage Organize Develop **Classify** Bewilder *Comfort* **Educate** Visualize *Advocate* Fashion Provide Shape Augment Believe Urge *Sanctify* Motivate Who Am I And What Am I Here For

Believing in our dreams often gives us the courage to act on them ...

—Marcia Wieder
CEO/Founder of *Dream University*
Author and Dream Coach

The Infinite Intelligence that lives within me knows the answers that I need and is revealing them to me now. I am grateful because everything I need is given to me.

Without deliberation, list three or more particular experiences, dating back from your early childhood, when you were completely focused on an activity or project, felt creative, enthusiastic, and had a sense of enjoyment and purpose.

____

____

____

____

____

____

____

____

____

My Purpose

I've come to believe that each of us has a personal calling that's as unique as a fingerprint, and that the best way to succeed is to discover what you love and then find a way to offer it to others in the form of service, working hard, and also allowing the energy of the universe to lead you.

O Magazine, September 2002
from "Laura Moncur's Motivational Quotations"

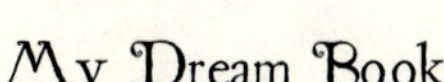

Observe who you were and how you felt in each instance. Are there common feelings and experiences among the events, happenings, or activities in which you were involved?

Classify any common feelings and experiences you had in these happenings or events. Write a generic summary using broad, concise statements (for example, "I felt creative or challenged").

____

____

____

____

____

____

____

____

____

____

____

____

____

My Reason for Being

You are not the momentary whim of a careless creator experimenting in the laboratory of life... You were made with a purpose.

Og Mandino

Discovering what your life is really all about will strongly impact the way you live and the choices you make. You will experience more fulfillment, enthusiasm, and peace when your goals line up with what truly motivates your heart. It is easy to be influenced and caught up in someone else's dream for your life. A dream must come from within, however, and be born from your true passions. With this in mind, consider your answers from the previous exercises. They can help you find the path from your passions to your purpose. Reflect on the content and begin writing freely about what your purpose might be. Meditate and reflect on what inspires and motivates you and gives your life a deeper sense of meaning.

____

____

____

____

____

____

____

____

Like most accomplishments, dreams are attained one little step at a time. Some dreams seem larger than life, and some dreams are as simple as wanting your closet organized. Owning our dreams may find us feeling a bit uncomfortable or embarrassed. But until we are brave enough to name the secret desires of our heart, they will most likely never be fulfilled.

> So … Come on … I Dare you.
> Decide what you want. It may look impossible, but hold your dream in your mind. Look for ways around any obstacles that you see. Believe that you deserve it and that it's possible for you. Believe in miracles. They do exist!
> —Modeled after the writing of author Jack Canfield as featured in *The Secret* by Rhonda Byrne

My Favorite Inspirational Quotes

Your true source of wealth consists of the ideas in your mind. You can have an idea worth millions of dollars. Your subconscious will give you the idea you seek.

—Dr. Joseph Murphy

When you open up to the potential of having what you want, you allow wonderful people and events to appear in your life.

—Marcia Wieder

I take me wherever I go. If I don't change, I will be who I have been.

—Kurt-Edouard Neubauer

To start the day with a conscious decision to be grateful, kind, gentle and patient with others helps to still the mind of my ego.

When you spend just one moment putting the interests of another soul above your own, that is the moment when God's presence can be felt most strongly.

—Gerald. J. Jampolsky, M.D.

… if your inward desire is to ultimately achieve a greater degree of success … then consider applying Watson's sage advice; shift what you're focusing on and see if you can, through increased activity, *"Double your rate of failure."*

—Michael S. Clouse

You can have more than one purpose in life, and you can do them together or do them sequentially, it doesn't matter, so long as you are pursuing them and not some other unimportant thing.

—Po Bronson

As you come across quotations that encourage and inspire you, take the time to jot them down on the lines below, referring to them often for motivation to believe in your dreams. Commit some to memory like you would an affirmation or scripture.

____

____

____

____

____

____

____

____

____

____

Inspirational Quotes

Section II: My Dream Journal

My Bucket List

The Things I Want to Do Before I Cross Over to the Other Side

The things that one most wants to do are the things that are probably most worth doing.

—Winifred Holtby

For Inspiration

When John Goddard, world-famous adventurer and speaker, was only fifteen years old he sat down and made what he called a *Life List*. On this list he wrote 127 goals that he hoped to attain during his lifetime. He wrote activities like seeing the Great Wall of China, visiting the Great Pyramids, learning to fly a plane and reading the entire *Encyclopedia Britannica*. By the time he was in his seventies he had achieved 109 of the goals written on that list. Goddard did not arrive at his goals based on the desires of his ego. He didn't believe in chasing exciting activities just for the sake of frivolous pleasure. He used these experiences to achieve what he considered a worthwhile end.

On the lines provided below, start a list of activities or experiences that you think would enrich your life. The kinds of events that most people might regret they never had the chance to do. This might be something as small as taking a cross-country vacation via a train or seeing the Eiffel tower. Return to this list often as you become more aware of dreams that belong on your *bucket list*.

____

____

____

____

____

____

____

____

____

____

____

What fears do I feel about my dreams?

____

____

____

What philosophies do I embrace that are limiting and holding me back from pursuing my dreams?

____

____

____

____

Who could I share my dreams with for accountability and support?

____

____

____

____

What are some small steps I could take toward pursuing my dreams?

____

____

____

____

An affirming faith thought or affirmation that can help overcome
my negative and limiting beliefs is:

____

____

____

I Am Thankful For...

On the lines below, list the experiences in your life that were significant accomplishments for which you can feel grateful today.

____

____

____

____

____

____

____

____

____

Affirmations and Faith Declarations

I am divinely guided to create my bucket list and believe that I will experience the wonderful moments I have listed. My *trust is in God, who richly gives me all I need for my enjoyment.*
(Paraphrase of 1 Timothy 6:17, NLT)

Using the above affirmation as an example, write your own affirmations or faith declarations according to your current needs and desires in this particular area.

Vision Page

Tape Or Glue Photos,

Magazine Cut-outs,

Sketch A Drawing Or

Use Other Visual Aids Here

My Health Dreams

For Inspiration

The following true stories are a reminder that there is a time to think outside the box, especially when dreaming in seemingly impossible situations. Whether or not you are a believer in alternative or holistic medicine, the following account will hopefully inspire you to cast aside any limiting thoughts you hold about health.

There are some health pioneers out there, like Dr. Richard Schulze and Reverend George Malkmus, who have had some amazing healings during their lifetimes and consequently have made bold statements about the healing abilities of the human body.

Richard Schulze wrote the book *There Are No Incurable Diseases*. A statement about health doesn't get much bolder than that! Considered an authority on natural healing, Richard's parents both died of heart attacks before he even reached fifteen years of age. By age sixteen, he was diagnosed himself with a genetic heart deformity considered incurable and was told by the age of twenty he would be dead. When the young Schulze heard someone who had the same surgery he was scheduled for had just died, he left the hospital and sought other means to heal his heart condition. And Richard Schulze did just that!

After curing himself without surgery through drastic changes made in his lifestyle and alternative medicine, he began a lifelong quest to help others. He teaches on the use of herbs and the basics of natural healing to empower people to help themselves heal. He created the American Botanical Pharmacy, and sells "industrial-strength, pharmaceutical, botanical extracts." His company also sells books, videos, and audiotapes teaching people how to take control of their health to create healing miracles.

Considered a radical and even an extremist, testimonials by his patients indicate his program may work. He believes that "All disease is caused by some type of blockage, whether it's lymphatic, digestive, nutritional, elimination, emotional, whatever. Free the blockage, let the energy flow, and healing begins immediately." For more information and inspiration, visit Dr. Schulze's website at http://www.herbdoc.com.

Reverend George Malkmus wrote the book *Why Christians Get Sick* after a tumor was found and later dissolved in his colon. He had watched his mom die of colon cancer and was convinced the chemo and radiation treatments had only contributed to her horrible death. Also, as a minister of twenty years, he had been at the bed-side of many of his church members and watched their devastating experiences with the traditional treatment of cancers. He had seen some of the most dedicated Christians, in spite of the prayers of many, grow worse and die when following traditional western medicine practices. He felt a lot of pressure to take the same route but instead turned to a friend, an evangelist in Texas named Lestor Roloff for help. Brother Roloff was known for being a "health-nut." Roloff's advice sounded strange but Malkmus decided to give it a try. He chose not to go the medical protocol, but instead change his diet radically to raw fruits, veggies and drink lots of freshly squeezed juice. Malkmus writes,

> Overnight I changed from a meat-centered, cooked and processed food diet with plenty of sugar desserts, to an all-raw diet with lots of carrot juice. I stayed on this total raw diet for approximately one year. I didn't eat any cooked food during that year … just raw fruits, raw vegetables and one to two quarts a day of freshly extracted, raw carrot juice. In less than one year, every physical problem I had been experiencing also disappeared!

My Health Dreams

Perhaps the biggest challenge to achieving your health dreams is in the way you were raised, the habits you've formed, and a possible lack of knowledge in alternative or holistic medicine. Creating good health is a lifetime endeavor. Making small changes in your lifestyle can help you improve and reach your health goals. I believe dreams are powerful and that one of the keys to realizing your health dreams is convincing your subconscious mind that not only can you achieve your dreams, but determine that you will do so. *May you prosper and be in health!*

My Dreams of Being Healthy

Begin with a few questions, taking an inventory of your health. How do you define good health? Are you willing to take responsibility for your own health and healing? Do you believe that good health can happen to you? The answers to these questions will give you a place to start when writing about your dreams for being healthy.

____

____

My Health Dreams

What fears do I feel about my dreams?

____

____

____

What philosophies do I embrace that are limiting and holding me
back from pursuing my dreams?

____

____

____

____

Who could I share my dreams with for accountability and support?

____

____

____

____

What are some small steps I could take toward pursuing my dreams?

____

____

____

____

An affirming faith-thought that can help overcome my negative and limiting beliefs is:

____

____

____

I Am Thankful For ...

On the lines below, list the things about your health for which you can feel grateful today.

____

____

____

____

____

____

____

____

____

____

My Health Dreams

Affirmations and Faith Declarations

The perfection of God is now being expressed through me. The idea of perfect health is now filling my subconscious mind. The image God has of me is a perfect image, and my subconscious mind recreates my body in perfect accordance with the perfect image held in the mind of God.

—Joseph Murphy, Ph.D., D.D.

Using the above affirmation as an example, write your own affirmations or faith declarations according to your current needs in this particular dream area.

____

____

____

____

____

____

____

____

____

____

Vision Page

Tape Or Glue Photos,

Magazine Cut-outs,

Sketch A Drawing Or

Use Other Visual Aids Here

My Dream Body

Many times the traditional size-8 woman is the least stylish and the most self-loathing, and the woman who is more voluptuous may be radiant, stylish and sexy because she is confident and doesn't hate what she sees every time she looks in the mirror.

—Isaac Mizrahi

For Inspiration

Nothing can seem more intimidating and impossible than the thought of attaining one's dream body. Before you begin to work this section, read this true, inspirational story about how one woman went for her dream body.

The Biggest Loser

As a startling chill descended upon my home, I began making preparations for the first fire of the winter season. Rummaging through the newspaper pile that had been collected for just such an occasion, my plan was to start a fire quickly. I became distracted however by the print and began glancing over the many stories, ads, and highlights. I found and skimmed one about a man who recovered from lung cancer using phytoplankton and thought, *Oh, I should cut this out and read it later.* I grabbed some scissors and quickly finished that job and then determined to resist further distractions and proceed with crumpling up the papers, placing them underneath the firewood.

But just as I was about to do that, I stopped dead in my tracks and stared at a picture of someone I recognized or *almost* recognized. I read the name. *I know this name*, I thought. It mentioned Fort Worth. I used to *live* in Fort Worth.

I stared a moment longer and was taken back to a baby shower that I was given almost nine years ago. I remembered a young girl, around eighteen years of age at the most, whose face was that of an angel and whose quiet presence, stylish clothing and fashionable eyewear struck and impressed me.

There was only one problem in my mind. Shelly, as her family called her, was overweight, and since I had never been happy with my own weight, I thought to myself, *Oh, how sad it is to see such a beautiful girl who is already overweight at such a young age.* I feared that her unusual loveliness would never be seen, remaining forever hidden behind the intricate, multi-layered identity of *fat*.

My thoughts returned to the photograph upon which I gazed in awe—a slender young woman with a look on her face that I could only describe as exuberant.

The newspaper article gave her name then began, "…of Fort Worth was crowned the winner of The Biggest Loser, NBC's weight-loss reality show, on Tuesday… (she), 26, snagged the $250,000 prize and will star in a milk mustache ad. She lost 110 pounds, 45 percent of her body weight, to weigh in at 132."

My eyes filled up with tears of joy for her and her family. I thought about Shelly's background: the challenges her family faced, including a broken home. At times she may have felt her life was filled with seemingly endless personal struggles. I was there when a relationship with her mom, a close friend of mine, became something she avoided. I recall that I had perceived Shelly as lacking in dating or social relationships one would normally expect for a young woman of her age.

But here she was smiling at me from the newspaper, looking

more gorgeous than I'd ever seen her. I excitedly *googled* her name and found an article, which gave this quote from her interview:

> Staying in the mental capacity of saying you're strong enough and you're worth it is a lot harder than even doing the physical workout…

I pondered her words. I felt grateful and happy for her, and rather profoundly I realized that my friend's daughter had learned something invaluable, more than just how to lose weight.

She had learned that great things really do begin in our minds with what may appear a seemingly impossible dream but with persistence, determination, and an eye-on-the-prize faith, we really can have what we expect and affirm for ourselves.

Yes, with a bright future that looks promisingly full, Shelly is slender and gorgeous now. I wonder if in retrospect she would say that her life really changed that moment she imagined herself thin and successful. The moment she made the decision to believe in, to follow, and to act on her dreams…

Dreams for My Body

As you begin to write about your *dream* body, ask yourself these questions. What misconceptions do I currently hold about my body? What do other people say about my weight or size? What do I need to accept about the way I look and what do I need to change? Are my dreams based on reality or on the expectations of a culture that only sees beauty in retouched photographs of already thin models in magazines?

____

____

____

____

What fears do I feel about my dreams?

What philosophies do I embrace that are limiting and holding me back from pursuing my dreams?

____

____

Who could I share my dreams with for accountability and support?

____

____

____

What are some small steps I could take toward pursuing my dreams?

____

____

____

An affirming faith-thought that can help overcome my negative and limiting beliefs is:

____

____

____

____

I Am Thankful For ...

On the lines below, write about your best features or characteristics of your physique for which you can feel grateful today.

____

____

____

____

____

____

____

____

____

____

____

____

My Dream Body

Affirmations and Faith Declarations

My entire body was formed by ingenious intellect with the ability to balance itself. The Divine presence within me possesses the knowledge and gives me the desire to care for, accept and be the best me I can be.

Using the above affirmation as an example, write your own affirmations or faith declarations about your dreams for your body.

____

____

____

____

____

____

____

____

____

____

____

Vision Page

Tape Or Glue Photos,

Magazine Cut-outs,

Sketch A Drawing Or

Use Other Visual Aids Here

Style

Scarves Evening *Wear* Business Funny *Sexy* Denim Budget-wear *Stylish* Complete Wardrobe *Swimwear* **Plaid** Stripes Jeans Straight-leg Frocks Designer Wear LINEN **Beads Ribbons Knitted Paper** Earrings Jewelry Handbags Wooden *Vinyl* Seashell Opal Cute CHIC Cork Lipstick Personal Style **Vintage** Fresh Classic *Ankle* Boots Bargain-buys Leather *See-through* Eyebrows *Black-and-white* Elegant Hosiery Shoes Crinoline Shorts Dresses *Cinched-waist* Eyeliner **Tailored** BEAUTIFUL Comfort Camisole CUFFED Jackets Skirt Bangs Silk Cashmere Feminine *Tweed* Flats *Skinny Jeans* Charm Bracelets Turtle-neck *Boots* Red Intimate-wear **Black Pumps** Brocade Lace Navy Short-sleeved Elbow-length Eye Shadow SPIKY Layered *Low-cut* Facial Floral Embellishments Pedicure Vertical Stripes Heels **Button-down Shirt** Athletic Wear *Spaghetti Straps* **Little Black Dress** Perfect Hem Length White Jeans *Cocktail* Earrings **Fashionable** Animal-print *Leather* Caftan Concealer Heeled Sandals **Glamorous** Peep-toe *Crisp* White Blouse Faux Fur Satin Sequins Metallic *Fabrics* Stunning **Blonde** ACCESSORIZE Wedge Sandals **Trench Coat** Black Rights Peek-a-boo Pearls Tote Bag *Black* Patent Strapless Barn Coat Plain Gold Hoops *Flamboyant* Diamond Studs

My Dream Style

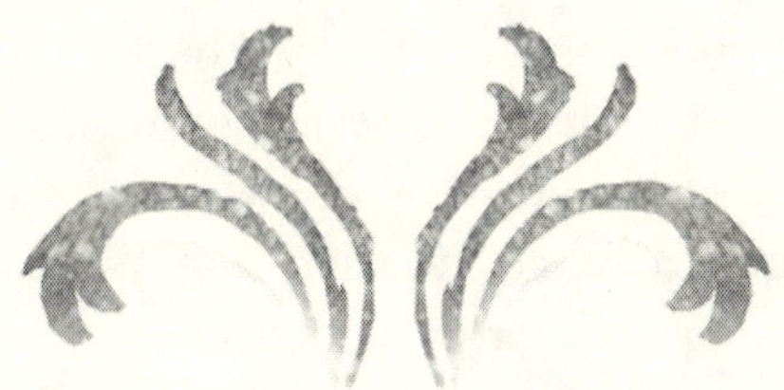

For Inspiration

Vivian Llodra is an *opinionated fashionista* according to *What Not to Wear's* Web site. She believes in looking good wherever she goes. Recently, Vivian wrote an article titled "From Ugly Duckling to Beautiful Swan," which tells the true story of Holly who appeared on *What Not to Wear*. According to those who nominated her, Holly was *in serious need of a self-confidence boost*. Holly may not have been too surprised that she was nominated once she was shown the secret footage they had taken for the show.

She realized she had been hiding behind her clothes. Avoiding anything that would draw attention to her, Holly admitted she'd gone through a time when she felt frumpy. Like many women, as their lives and ages change, she'd gained weight. Part of what she'd gone through was giving up her dream of being a professional ballet dancer.

She'd begun to dress in neutrals, perhaps symbolizing that her life was stuck in neutral.

At one point when Stacy and Clinton from the show were working with Holly, she became adamant that she didn't *see the ballerina she once was*. Stacy's rebuttal was that Holly had to let go of what she was in the past so that she could become who she *will* be.

After tossing most of Holly's wardrobe, she is sent out to shop. One thing that really caught my eye about Holly's experience was that Stacy and Clinton gave her affirmations to repeat to herself throughout the day in order to boost her confidence. Walking into a large store, Holly felt overwhelmed by the store size. She repeated her affirmation: *I will feel the way I do when I dance.*

Clinton and Stacy were not impressed as Holly continually chose colors that were not flattering to her skin tone, washing her out. As the shopping continued into day two, she began to realize how negative she'd been throughout the process, and that *negative* summarized the way she's viewed her life. Amazingly, Holly had a breakthrough during the process and was able to appreciate herself again, seeing that there really wasn't anything wrong with her body. She decided to focus on positive steps she could take to change her outlook. Holly then took herself and her new outfits to her hair makeover.

After some wonderful changes, including a haircut with bangs, she really surprised everyone working with her by her transformation. Leaving her neutral colors behind, Holly attended her party back home in a stylish, magenta-colored dress. Everyone thought she looked great, and her family seemed delighted with her style makeover.

The amazing thing about Holly's transformation experience was her realization that her clothing style, including her hair, was reflective of what was really going on with her. She had stopped valuing herself because her life had taken a different direction career-wise. Because of loving friends who nominated her, Holly was confronted by her style choices and what they indicated about her. She embraced the significance this opportunity afforded and chose to recognize she could move past her disillusionment and break through her self-imposed confinements. By taking a realistic look at her style, she was able to reclaim her self-worth and began to celebrate the beautiful person that she is.

The Style of My Dreams

There is something that you will do every day of your life. You did it today, you did it yesterday, and you will do it tomorrow. You will do this even when you forget to brush your teeth or when you are sick in the hospital. *Today and every other day for the rest of your life, you will get dressed!*

This is an area of importance that can be overlooked. The way you wear your hair, the clothes you choose, and even your accessories are expressions of how you see yourself. This exercise will take one or two days, and I feel confident you'll learn something about yourself that will be helpful for the rest of your life.

If you have a lot of clothes in your closet, create five totally different styles of outfits to try on. If you need to go to a store, pick one that has a variety of designers like Macy's or Dillard's. Again, pick out at least five totally different looks to try on. Take a friend along to take pictures and allow yourself to see how you feel in each of those looks. Search the Internet and visit sites like http://www.wikihow.com/Category:Fashion-Styles.

Another activity that will inspire you to make improvements in your style will be to organize your closet. Take a day where you try on everything you own and toss those things that you haven't worn in over a year. The only exception to this might be an evening gown, tuxedo or other special-event outfits. Taking everything out and putting back only what you need in categories will simplify your daily life. Try putting pants with pants, dresses with dresses and tops with tops. Organizing your clothing by colors is something I borrowed from my mother-in-law. When my closet is arranged in this manner, I love the way everything looks and how easy it is to mix and match.

Which style fits you best? Romantic? Modern? Classic? Chic? Conservative? Sporty? Loud? Professional? Preppy? Glamorous? Casual? Vintage? Trendsetter? Flashy?

____

____

____

Which style was the most flattering? Which one felt like you the most?

____

____

What colors have I been told I look good in but am afraid to wear?

____

____

When I think of style, my fashion icons are:

____

____

Jewelry that I dream of:

____

____

Write any additional thoughts you have about your dream style. Perhaps you have seen some dreams outfits or accessories at the local

My Dream Style

stores or online that you would like to own some day. Refer to the word list on the previous page for ideas.

What fears do I feel about my dreams?

____

____

____

____

What philosophies do I embrace that are limiting and holding me back from pursuing my dreams?

____

____

____

Who could I share my dreams with for accountability and support?

____

____

____

____

What are some small steps I could take toward pursuing my dreams?

____

____

____

My Dream Style

An affirming faith thought that can help overcome my negative and
limiting beliefs is:

____

____

____

I Am Thankful For ...

On the lines below, list the things about your wardrobe for which
you can feel grateful today. Name some of your favorite outfits that
you feel you look good in, or perhaps the clothes you wear at home
on the days you don't have to go out.

____

____

____

____

____

____

____

____

____

Affirmations and Faith Declarations

I believe and declare that I am beautiful and charismatic, exuding confidence, love, and joy to others when we meet or I walk into the room. I know what clothes and colors look best on me, and my style and attitude reflect the beautiful, amazing person I am on the inside.

—Affirmation by Mashelle James

Following the example above, write your own faith-building statements on the lines below.

____

____

____

____

____

____

____

____

____

____

____

My Dream Style

Vision Page

Tape Or Glue Photos,

Magazine Cut-outs,

Sketch A Drawing Or

Use Other Visual Aids Here

Education and Career Dreams

Instead of seeing yourself as … famous … see yourself inspiring countless people with your work … Feel how that activity enriches … not only your life but that of countless others. Being an opening through which energy flows from the unmanifested Source of all life through you for the benefit of all.

—Eckhart Tolle

For Inspiration

When I was a little girl of preschool age, I remember my mother attending college. I didn't really understand what that meant, but I recall the feeling of excitement I caught from her as she began her education. I was always thrilled when I was allowed to go to the campus with her. She would meet with other students, and they would sit in a circle, having discussions, laughing, and writing. I always liked going with her to school or to study. She looked happy and actively engaged in what she was doing. Sometimes she would let me do an educational activity associated with her coursework.

After I started grade school, I realized my mom was studying to become a teacher. In spite of my father's terminal illness, she pressed on driving forty-five minutes each way to her classes. I recall her having tears at times when leaving us to go to the campus. I always wondered why my Dad drove so slowly to take me to school. My mom knew my daddy was dying, but of course, I did not. Nor did I know that she, with little family encouragement, without a high school education, and against the greatest odds, was daring to go for her dream. She was determined to make a better way of life for us.

Here is her story in her own words; may it remind you to dream big about your own future.

Dreams By Marge Ellington

Sometimes in the beginning, a dream may be just a small stirring, a faint idea. The thought will come to mind again and again, always seemingly impossible. Something inside, though, will grow stronger, a force that will not let go. As you think about the idea, you will begin to see a way to make it happen. It will become a possibility, and a desire will build inside until you see it come to pass. The idea will not go away. You will be reminded by something persistently leading you in that direction.

As a child, the classroom was a magical place. I could hardly wait each day to be in my seat and hear what my teachers had to say. I loved learning. My education in the classroom, however, was cut short. Circumstances beyond my control got in the way, and I found myself married at fourteen years of age.

On September 1, the yellow school bus passed me by. I remember standing in the yard watching it go out of sight. It was an overwhelming disappointment. I recognized that perhaps I'd never step my foot in a classroom again. I had finished the eighth grade. As far as I could see in my future, a formal education was over and done with.

I saw teenagers going on and graduating from high school, and I knew something was terribly missing in my life. Life has a way of pushing you on to the next level. I had begun a course I had to finish. The dream never left me to get a high school diploma, and I knew my life was on a course I had to finish. I learned to daydream—by

                    Education and Career Dreams

that I refer to imagining in your mind the dream becoming a reality. You can see it happening as you are going through the process.

I lived through the birth of two wonderful children and the end of a long first marriage. Several years later, I found myself married again to a wonderful man, Buddy, and gave birth to a sweet baby girl. Shortly after, I was working in a dress factory making minimum wage when tragedy struck. I learned that my husband had a disease they thought was muscular dystrophy.

Although he was limited in his ability to work, he could drive a tractor. He farmed watermelons and raised cattle. With me working, he made a crop in the summer, and we lived fairly well. It was during the month of June, and my husband provided the daily care for our baby girl. He had forty-three acres of land leased for watermelons and should have been plowing that day. I came home and saw he had not plowed. I asked our little four-year-old daughter, "What is Daddy doing?" She said, "He's sleeping."

The next day I made an appointment to see a cardiologist. After the test, Dr. Brown—I will never forget his name (it was also my maiden name)—asked me to come into his office. Without compassion or any display of emotion, he said, "Mrs. Boyd, your husband has six months to live, perhaps a year." My husband and I never spoke of it; there were no tears. Instead, an overwhelming determination came over me. As we left the office, I said to Buddy, "I'll make the watermelon crop."

The next day my husband took me to ten acres of sandy loam soil. We got on the tractor, and he taught me how to turn the tractor around, and I began to lay off rows to plant watermelon seed. He and my little daughter would sit at the end of the rows, and I would plow all day. These were the most wonderful days of my life, as I spent them with my husband and our young daughter. Eventually we marketed over a million pounds of watermelons. I heard about the GED (General Educational Development certificate), and so I took the test. With God as my witness, I scored above average on it. I could now go to a community college. In spite of the reality of our sad future bearing down upon me, I had no time to feel sorry for myself. I had a job to do. The dream (once seemingly impossible) was becoming a reality. I visited the local campus and asked, "Can I go to college?" They said, "Yes!" They would support and encourage me all the way. I had dreamed for twenty-four years of this becoming a reality; never did I imagine I would bypass high school and move into higher education.

Now, the fight—how did I do it? My family (especially my mother) began to discourage me with, "You can't leave an unhealthy husband and little girl and be gone three days a week. Besides, you never set a day in a high school classroom!"

I told my husband, "All I need is your support and belief that I can do it." He told me to start that first semester, and he would push me all the way. Each morning, he put his arms around me, holding me before I went on my way. At night, I held my little girl and dreamed my way through those years. I would not allow myself to think that I could fail. I would visualize myself as a teacher with my daughter and I having the same vacation, being with her every day. I knew I had missed much during the first four years of her life. I had no choice but to work and help support us. My incredible older daughter took up the slack and helped care for her little sister. She was fourteen and half years older. She was faithful to help and deserves applause for supporting us on our way to becoming who we are today.

The first semester I was on the dean's list. Though my family and I suffered hardships, we experienced the joy and excitement of a dream coming true. I enrolled in a music class, and we were able to buy a piano. My young daughter would sit beside me when I practiced. She would listen as her daddy and I would play the old Bob Wills's fiddle tunes like "San Antonio Rose." While he played a wonderful country fiddle, we loved and lived as I had dreamed. In four years, I walked out of the University of North Texas with a Bachelor of Science degree and an endorsement to teach kindergarten.

My husband lived two more years and saw me teach almost a year before he went to be with the Lord. I taught over twenty years

   Education and Career Dreams

in elementary school. I also completed many hours toward a master's degree in elementary education.

Dare to dream the impossible dream. I am living proof it can and will happen. Don't limit yourself and settle for too little. Many people say to themselves, "It's too hard!" That's a cop-out. If it wasn't hard, it would not be worth it. God will make a way; he does and he did, but I had to put feet to my prayer and believe that I would find a way to do it.

Do dreams come true? Bet your life on it. Dare to dream! It can come true.

What Do I Want to Be When I Grow Up?

Spend some time brainstorming on the lines below about your education and dream career. You might think your dream career would make you a celebrity; however, after you explore and discover what your real purpose is, you may find that you don't have to be a star to have a fulfilling and rewarding career. You may be surprised to find that a less glamorous job will be the one that really offers what brings you joy and a sense of purpose.

Be open-minded and think outside the box. However, don't limit yourself. Say, for example, that you may have loved school and thought that teaching would be your field. You may find that your dream job will be in a related area but perhaps not exactly that position. Do some research and spend time exploring your interests, talents, and abilities. Ask your friends and family in what area they feel you have talent or the type of situations in which you shine. They may not always be helpful, and don't let them limit you. Yet they may surprise you with their responses. You could even stay in your current line of work but move into a different niche and find great improvement in your career.

____

____

____

____

____

____

____

Education and Career Dreams

____

____

____

____

____

____

____

What fears do I feel about my dreams?

____

____

____

What philosophies do I embrace that are limiting and holding me
back from pursuing my dreams?

____

____

____

Who could I share my dreams with for accountability and support?

____

What are some small steps I could take toward pursuing my dreams?

____

____

____

An affirming faith thought or affirmation that can help overcome my negative and limiting beliefs is:

____

____

____

I Am Thankful For…

On the lines below, list the things about your current job, educational background, or career training that are blessings. Look at the obstacles you may have already overcome for which you can feel thankful.

____

____

____

____

____

____

____

____

____

____

____

____

Affirmations and Faith Declarations

I am employed doing a job I truly enjoy.
One that utilizes my gifts, skills,
and natural talents. It allows me
to use the creative genius within.
The people I work with respect me
and I show them respect in return.
I am financially blessed and out of
my abundance, am a blessing to others.

Modeled after an affirmation
by Louise Hay in *You Can Heal Your Life*

Using the above affirmation as an example, write your own affirmations or faith declarations according to your current dreams for your education and career.

Education and Career Dreams

____

____

____

____

____

____

Enjoyment of what you are doing combined with a goal or vision
that you work toward becomes enthusiasm.

—Eckhart Tolle

Vision Page

Tape Or Glue Photos,

Magazine Cut-outs,

Sketch A Drawing Or

Use Other Visual Aids Here

Vision Page

Tape Or Glue Photos,

Magazine Cut-outs,

Sketch A Drawing Or

Use Other Visual Aids Here

Abundance

Leave your country, your people and your father's household and go to the land I will show you. I will make you into a great nation and I will bless you; I will make your name great, and you will be a blessing.

Genesis 12:1–8 (NIV)

The quotes below suggest that in order to attract abundance, we must be abundance minded. If we unknowingly set our expectations on being poor, we may even lose what we have, as shortage will be our anticipation. You've heard it said, "We reap what we sow." Live with a scarcity mentality, and you will likely have scarcity. Even wealthy people can live like they are poor. You've probably heard the stories and know that some rich people are known for being misers. The more they get, the more afraid they are of losing. This is because they did not shed their deprivation mentality when becoming rich. They live and feel poor and believe they are doing the right thing. The saddest thing about this situation is that they lose the opportunity to be a blessing to others.

Being wealthy can give one the chance to bless others in amazing ways. Being wealthy should not be considered an evil thing, nor should we esteem poverty as more admirable than wealth. The first secret to becoming rich is to make the decision. Decide that it is permissible and that you are going to become wealthy. Read books that build your confidence and help you set your resolve to receive the blessings God has for you. Create a contract committing yourself to being blessed and to be a blessing. Review it on a daily basis until it becomes a part of you.

Begin to look at yourself as wealthy, expressing gratitude for what you already have. Feel grateful as if you have already attained great wealth. Eventually you will attract abundance and wealth into your life. See yourself taking your wealth and being a blessing to the world.

…ye have not, because ye ask not

James 4:2 (KJV)

Education and Career Dreams

Give and it will be given to you. Good measure, pressed down, shaken together, running over, will be put into your lap.

Luke 6:38 (NRSV)

The source of all abundance is not outside you. It is part of who you are … start by acknowledging and recognizing abundance without … acknowledgment of that abundance that is all around you awakens the dormant within … abundance comes only to those who already have it.

—Eckhart

For to the one who has, more will be given, and from the one who has not, even what he has will be taken away.

Mark 4:25 (ESV)

My Financial Dreams

It's been said that people tend to wind up exactly where they belong in life. That's because we live what we know. Without new knowledge, we can't change.

—David Bach

For Inspiration

Here is a visual aid that Jack Canfield suggests using as featured in *The Secret* by Rhonda Byrne. He tells an incredible story of how he was challenged by a mentor to write what seemed like a ridiculously large amount of money on a check and place it where he would see it morning and night. At the time, $100,000 seemed completely out of reach and he had no idea how he could make that amount of money. He had written a book but it had been rejected by publishers. One day as he was passing by one of the supermarket tabloids, *National Enquirer,* he thought if readers of that tabloid knew about his book, they might go out and buy it. He thought about how wonderful it would be if his book was advertised and sold to 400,000 readers.

About six weeks later he was speaking to an audience of teachers. Afterwards a woman came up and told him she'd like to interview him. It just so happened that she was a freelance writer who sold her stories to the same magazine publication he'd thought about a six weeks before. The rest is history. The amount of money he had made at the end of the year was over $92,000 dollars. After this his wife said, *If this works for $100,000 do you think it would work for a million?* He thought it was worth a try. The results, he testifies were miraculous. When his publisher wrote him a check for the first *Chicken Soup for the Soul* book, Canfield says he put a smiley face on it because it was the first check he'd written for a million dollars. This is another example of how the power of the subconscious mind mixed with faith, hope, and gratitude are not to be underrated.

Below are blank checks. Start with a number that seems out of reach but within your ability to imagine being real. For example, if you need fifty thousand dollars to get out of debt, you could write the check for fifty thousand. The next check you write will be more, I bet!

<table>
<tr><td>1st Bank of Abundance</td><td>Date   /   /</td></tr>
<tr><td>Pay __________________________________</td><td>$__________________</td></tr>
<tr><td colspan="2">To the Order of ____DOLLARS</td></tr>
<tr><td colspan="2">SIGNED: ____</td></tr>
<tr><td colspan="2">111 111111|: 777 777777   Owner of the Cattle on a Thousand Hills</td></tr>
</table>

<table>
<tr><td>1st Bank of Abundance</td><td>Date   /   /</td></tr>
<tr><td>Pay __________________________________</td><td>$__________________</td></tr>
<tr><td colspan="2">To the Order of ____DOLLARS</td></tr>
<tr><td colspan="2">SIGNED: ____</td></tr>
<tr><td colspan="2">111 111111|: 777 777777   The Universe</td></tr>
</table>

My Financial Dreams

<table>
<tr><td colspan="2">1st Bank of Abundance</td><td>Date   /   /</td></tr>
<tr><td>Pay ____</td><td colspan="2">$________________</td></tr>
<tr><td colspan="3">To the Order of ___________________________________DOLLARS</td></tr>
<tr><td colspan="3">SIGNED: ___________________________________</td></tr>
<tr><td colspan="2">111 111111|: 777 777777</td><td>The Great I AM</td></tr>
</table>

Becoming wealthy one day may seem completely out of the question for most people. It may appear like a mystical quest that is reserved for only a sacred few. Many attempt get-rich-quick schemes, only to walk away disappointed and disillusioned that they will ever have any serious money. The truth is that no matter your age or your income, you can decide to improve your financial future today. With some realistic goal-setting, simple planning, and consistent discipline, you can turn your financial life around.

You can begin today with a simple goal. Decide to save the $4.00 every day that you would normally spend on a coffee drink or candy bar and soft drink. At the end of each week, place that money in a savings account at 5% interest, and in 30 years it will grow to around $100,000. This amounts to saving around $120 a month. This may seem a large amount at first, but the day will come when it seems small. As you write your financial dreams, include answers to the questions below as you begin to dream about your financial future.

1. What are a few things I could give up in order to save money on a daily basis?

2. How much money can I begin to save now?

3. What is my savings goal for five years?

4. What is my savings goal for ten years?

5. What might be a realistic goal for twenty years?

____

____

____

____

____

____

____

____

____

____

What fears do I feel about my dreams?

____

____

____

My Financial Dreams

What philosophies do I embrace that are limiting and holding me back from pursuing my dreams?

____

____

____

____

Who could I share my dreams with for accountability and support?

____

____

____

____

What are some small steps I could take toward pursuing my dreams?

____

____

An affirming faith thought that can help overcome my negative and limiting beliefs is:

____

____

____

____

Money Making Ideas
(Dream Big–Brainstorm Big)

Ideas I have for books:

____

____

Invention ideas:

____

____

Business ideas:

____

____

Profitable hobby ideas:

____

____

Investment ideas:

____

____

Real Estate ideas:

____

____

Internet ideas:

____

____

My Financial Dreams

Fundraising ideas:

____

____

Ideas for my personal finances: (education funds, insurance plans, stocks and bonds, trust funds, IRAs, certificates of deposits [CDs], savings plan)

____

____

____

I Am Thankful For ...

On the lines below, list the things about your current financial situation for which you can feel grateful today.

____

____

____

____

____

____

____

Affirmations and Faith Declarations

I know and believe that my hidden talents and the ability to release them will bring wealth and abundance into my life.

Using the above affirmation as an example, write your own affirmations or faith declarations about your dreams for your financial future.

____

____

____

____

____

____

____

____

____

____

____

____

Vision Page

Tape Or Glue Photos,

Magazine Cut-outs,

Sketch A Drawing Or

Use Other Visual Aids Here

Classic Chic Trendy Luxurious *Beautiful* Country Urban **Metropolitan** Beatnik Chic **Parisian** *Oceanfront* Lakefront Log Cabin Mountainside Creekside **Modern** *Colonial* **Southwestern Tuscan Spanish Style Stucco Pueblo Brick** *Wood Spacious* **Cozy** Ranch Style **Cute Beach House Pier And Beam Slab Expansive** Renovated **Light And** *Airy* Expensive Bamboo **Garden Mosaic Tile** *European* **Elegant** *Gracious* **Asian Hand-painted Pine** Rock **Stone Chippendale Conventional Wrap-around** Porch **Lcony Terrace Formal** *Renaissance* **Medieval Contemporary** Marble Mahogany Granite Ceramic Porcelain Laminate Antique Fine-looking Iron Romantic White-wash **Crown** *Molding* **Depression Era Corian New England Classical** *Elgance* **Whimsy Charming** *Contemporary* **Fashionable Leather** *Exquisite* **Delicate Geometric Raw** *Veneer* **Fabric** *Archetypal* **Hip Countryside Fresh** *Medieval* **Rare** *Appealing* **Modish Restored**

My Dream Home

For Inspiration

In *The Secret* by Rhonda Byrne, John Assaraf shares a personal fairy tale surrounding his dream home. At one point in his life, being a believer in the law of attraction, he wanted to put its principles into practice. He made what many refer to as a vision board and put pictures of dream things on the board. I imagine so he would see them frequently, embedding the suggestion deeper into his subconscious mind.

Later, as John and his family were preparing to move, they put everything, including furniture, and boxes full of their belongings into storage. Five years and three moves later, they bought a house, and after a year of renovations, they moved in and finally brought their possessions out of storage.

One day, his five-and-a-half-year-old son came into his office and saw boxes labeled "Vision Boards." As his son began asking what a vision board was, John thought it easier to show him than try to explain it on a kindergarten level.

He opened the box, and inside was a vision board containing a picture of a house he'd dreamt of five years earlier. He was shocked when he realized it wasn't just a picture of a house he had liked. It was a picture of the very house he bought, renovated, and was now living in. Tears began to run down his face as he finally understood how powerful visualization is. He had bought his very dream home and did not even know it until that moment.

Completing this section may require research on your part but will
be well worth your time in the end.

Interior Features:

____

____

Floor Coverings:

____

____

Bathroom:

____

____

Closets:

____

____

Kitchen:

____

____

Appliances:

____

____

My Dream Home

Bedrooms:

____

____

Exterior Features:

____

____

Style:

____

____

Parking:

____

____

Lot Description:

____

____

Number of Stories:

____

____

____

Yard/Grounds:

____

____

Lot Size:

____

____

Utilities:

____

____

Heating:

____

____

Cooling:

____

____

Water:

____

____

Location
Amenities:

____

____

____

Special Features:

____

____

____

What philosophies do I embrace that are limiting and holding me
back from pursuing my dreams?

____

____

____

Who could I share my dreams with for accountability and support?

____

____

____

What are some small steps I could take toward pursuing my dreams?

____

____

____

An affirming faith thought that can help overcome my negative and limiting beliefs is:

____

____

____

I Am Thankful For ...

On the lines below, list the things about your current shelter or home for which you can feel grateful today. Return to this list and make additions any time you are feeling unhappy about your current living situation.

____

____

____

____

____

____

My Dream Home

____

____

____

____

____

____

Affirmations and Faith Declarations

I live in the home of my dreams. It has the space and amenities
I need in which to live life to the fullest. The style and location
are both perfect and I enjoy creating a living environment in
which I blossom.

Using the above affirmation as an example, write your own affirmations or faith declarations about the dreams you have discovered for
your home.

____

____

____

____

My Dream Home

Vision Page

Tape Or Glue Photos,

Magazine Cut-outs,

Sketch A Drawing Or

Use Other Visual Aids Here

Vision Page

Tape Or Glue Photos,

Magazine Cut-outs,

Sketch A Drawing Or

Use Other Visual Aids Here

My Dream Home

Vision Page

Tape Or Glue Photos,

Magazine Cut-outs,

Sketch A Drawing Or

Use Other Visual Aids Here

Vision Page

Tape Or Glue Photos,

Magazine Cut-outs,

Sketch A Drawing Or

Use Other Visual Aids Here

Vision Page

Tape Or Glue Photos,

Magazine Cut-outs,

Sketch A Drawing Or

Use Other Visual Aids Here

Vision Page

Tape Or Glue Photos,

Magazine Cut-outs,

Sketch A Drawing Or

Use Other Visual Aids Here

Sofas Streamlined *Look* **Cambelback** Vanderbyl Color Texture *Clarence* Housegold Tassels Triangular *Valance* Busy Patterns **Daybed** Family-size Sofa *Sheer* Curtains **Bright** White Raoul Textiles *Regency Revival* Chaise John Robsaw *Rogers & Goffigon* Raw Material Upholstery Sea Coral Pattern Formal **Setting** Intricately Drawn Lattice *Floral Print* Faux-suede High-backed Settee Modern **Sheraton** Sofa Pillow-back Sofa Chairs Woven **Plaid** Silk Moss FRINGER Geometric Striped **Velvet** Manuel Canovas *Matelasse* Fabricscorduroy Satin Embossed *Velvet* Crewel Ottomons Dessin Fournir Modern Authentic Piece *Love Seat* BUNSCHWIG & FILS Historical Eras Cotton Print Scaled Block Fring *Osborne & Little* Cowtan & Tout John Rosselli Cotton Chintz Single-welt Cord Bennison Chairs CLUB CHAIR Benches Wing Chair **Ralph Lauren** Home Window **Treatments** Retro Grey Watkins Paisley *Vertical* STRIPE Solo Armchair Slipcovers Furniture Construction ROMAN SHADE Dining Chairs *Covered* In Solids Chandelier Blue-and-white **Fabric** Candy-striping Faux Leopard Print Solid-colored Patterned Floral Floor Runner **Blanket** Scroll-shaped Pillow Deep Button Indentations TROPICAL Splendor **Treen-themed** Serving **Table** Pink-and-white Check **Tablecloths** Bold Stripes Corner Chair Trestle Bench Zebra Stripes *Decorative* Hardware Draperies **Black Chintz** Cornice Curtains On Rings Folding Screens *Upholstered* Headboards

       The Furnishings of My Dreams

The Furnishings of My Dreams

For Inspiration

A few years back, I was looking through magazines and found a picture featuring red bedroom furniture. I was struck by how much I liked furniture in the scarlet red and later found myself pulling the pictures out and placing them in a notebook. Several months later as I was looking at my bedroom furniture, it dawned on me that the room was sadly lacking in color. I remembered the photo from the home fashion magazine and pulled it out. *Why not paint my bedroom furniture that beautiful color of red?*, I thought. I went to Home Depot and found the right paint and began my project.

Within no time I had completed the project and, after purchasing two red pillows to go on the bed, my bedroom was transformed. If you would have asked me six months before that time what I could have done to have made my bedroom a better place for me, I would have said *buy furniture*. But making a major purchase (I hate to shop) sounded totally stressful at the time, and I just wasn't interested. Inspired by furniture in the magazines, I was able to make improvements in my bedroom quickly in an easy, inexpensive manner.

Designers, brand names or stores where I would like to shop for home furnishings:

____

____

____

Styles that interest me:

____

____

My favorite magazines for dreaming:

____

____

Colors schemes that catch my eye:

____

____

Fabrics and materials that appeal to me:

____

____

The Furnishings of My Dreams

Using the descriptive words from the previous page if needed, journal about the dreams you have for enhancing your home.

Vision Page

Tape Or Glue Photos,

Magazine Cut-outs,

Sketch A Drawing Or

Use Other Visual Aids Here

The Furnishings of My Dreams

Vision Page

Tape Or Glue Photos,

Magazine Cut-outs,

Sketch A Drawing Or

Use Other Visual Aids Here

Vision Page

Tape Or Glue Photos,

Magazine Cut-outs,

Sketch A Drawing Or

Use Other Visual Aids Here

The Furnishings of My Dreams

Vision Page

Tape Or Glue Photos,

Magazine Cut-outs,

Sketch A Drawing Or

Use Other Visual Aids Here

Vision Page

Tape Or Glue Photos,

Magazine Cut-outs,

Sketch A Drawing Or

Use Other Visual Aids Here

The Furnishings of My Dreams

Vision Page

Tape Or Glue Photos,

Magazine Cut-outs,

Sketch A Drawing Or

Use Other Visual Aids Here

My Dream Car

For Inspiration

How My Husband Acquired His First Car

When Michael was eighteen, like a lot of kids his age, he was without wheels. Having been awarded an academic scholarship, he was planning to attend college later that fall to study engineering. He was not employed and therefore had no money to purchase a vehicle. Owning a car seemed absolutely impossible to him at the time.

One day his next-door neighbor knocked on the door. He said, "I am being transferred with the navy to another naval base, and I have an extra car. Would you like to buy it?" Michael told him, "Oh, I'd love to, but I don't have any money." The guy said, "Well, I'm selling it really cheap." To which Michael replied, "Really, I'd love to, but I don't have a job, and I don't have any money." The guy said, "No, problem, I can get you a job. I have a second job at a beverage store, and since I'm leaving, they need someone to take my place."

Michael enthusiastically agreed to the arrangement. He went and applied the next day, and the day after that he started working. The man gave him time to pay off the car, and within a month he was the proud owner of an old, new car.

This true story is a reminder that sometimes a way is made when there seems no way. Sometimes what you need or desire may materialize as if out of thin air, so always remember to expect the unexpected. *The sky is the limit!*

The Car of My Dreams

Want a new car but not sure what that car looks like? Maybe you have short-term dreams for a car that's affordable now and long-term goals to own a more expensive car in the future. If you need a car or if cars are just your thing, then certain words will create images in your mind of your dream car. What is the body, make, or model of your dreams? Which of these words create a pleasant mental image for you?

- Horsepower
- Transmission Type
- Engineering
- Domestic
- Import
- Coupe
- Sedan
- SUV
- Truck
- Van
- Mini-van

What is the image you seek?

____

____

Style: Sleek, muscle, luxury, convertible, color, interior:

Accessories: Spoilers, fog lights, air dams, sunroof, moonroof, pinstriping, wheels, and tires:

____

____

____

Below is my friend Heather's dream car.

Maybe you know your dream car already. Could it be a '68 Camaro—royal blue metallic, ground effects, spoiler, aluminum slot mags, and Michelin tires with charcoal leather interior, tinted windows, and a 350 four-bolt main with a turbo-hydramatic 400 and a sound system to live for?

____

____

____

____

____

____

____

____

What philosophies do I embrace that are limiting and holding me back from pursuing my dreams?

____

____

____

Who could I share my dreams with for accountability and support?

____

____

____

____

What are some small steps I could take toward pursuing my dreams?

____

____

____

An affirming faith thought that can help overcome my negative and limiting beliefs is:

____

____

My Dream Car

I Am Thankful For ...

On the lines below, list the things about your current means of transportation for which you can feel grateful. It may just be that you have *wheels,* as it is always good to focus on the positive attributes about the cars we currently own. Be grateful and then be thankful for the nicer vehicle that will replace it some day.

Affirmations and Faith Declarations

I am blessed at all times with the means of transportation that
I need.

Using the above affirmation as an example, write your own
affirmations or faith declarations about your current auto needs
as if they were already met. Also write about your dreams for
your future vehicles.

Vision Page

Tape Or Glue Photos,

Magazine Cut-outs,

Sketch A Drawing Or

Use Other Visual Aids Here

Vision Page

Tape Or Glue Photos,

Magazine Cut-outs,

Sketch A Drawing Or

Use Other Visual Aids Here

My Dreams of Friendship

For Inspiration

I still remember when Mashelle and I met. I had tiptoed into her bedroom, and she smiled at me from behind her crib bars like no one had ever smiled at me before. When she looked at me that day, there was a spark of joy I'd never experienced in an adult's eyes. I was probably not even four years old, and she was less than year. We have literally been friends ever since.

I've reminisced on that moment many times over the years as our lives have taken some great twists and some very difficult turns. We were privileged to have had the chicken pox together, the time spent in matching nightgowns. Unfortunately, Mashelle watched me grow up fatherless when illness took mine, and I watched her become an object in a dreadful custody tug-of-war that impacted both our lives with lasting effects.

Mashelle is my sister's daughter, and we're only three years apart.

We have spent many holidays, vacations, and other significant occasions together. We've been each other's *maid of honor* and held each other's hand, praying silently as the other labored to give birth. We've had a few moments where we didn't understand each other, and many times when we were the only one who knew the difficulties the other was facing. We have rejoiced with each other in the good times as if the blessed moments were our own.

Mashelle is more than a friend; she is family, but our friendship bond is what has kept us close all these years. Now my business partner, she encourages me to believe in myself when I have lost confidence and shares my passion for inspiring others. The amazing thing about our friendship is the unconditional love and respect that we have for each other. To this very day, when she smiles at me my spirits lift, and no matter what my circumstances, I am taken back to a moment spent with an amazingly joyful toddler whose lifetime of friendship has brought me so much happiness.

My Friendships

On the lines below, write freely about any needs or improvements you would like to see in your current friendships. List any changes you would like to make in those relationships, and describe the new acquaintances or bonds that you would like to form. Perhaps this will be a place where you journal about broken relationships and any changes you could make within yourself. Since we make ourselves vulnerable in friendships, we sometimes get hurt. Perhaps you have some friends you need to forgive and could use this as an opportunity to explore that more.

____

____

____

   My Dreams of Friendship

____

____

____

____

____

____

What philosophies do I embrace that are limiting and holding me
back from pursuing my dreams?

____

____

____

____

Who could I share my dreams with for accountability and support?

____

____

____

What are some small steps I could take toward pursuing my dreams?

____

An affirming faith thought that can help overcome my negative and limiting beliefs is:

____

____

____

I Am Thankful For…

On the lines below, write about your current friendships. Consider friends you can count on in both the good times and the bad whose friendship is meaningful and for which you are grateful today. Also you could write about those persons that you may not consider close friends, like those you work with, who make your life a nicer place with their smile, humor, or support.

____

____

____

____

____

____

____

My Dreams of Friendship

____

____

____

____

____

____

Affirmations and Faith Declarations

My friendships are divinely appointed, and my friends are trustworthy and love me unconditionally.

Using the above affirmation as an example, write your own affirmations or faith declarations about your current needs for friendship as if they were already met.

____

____

____

____

____

____

Vision Page

Tape Or Glue Photos,

Magazine Cut-outs,

Sketch A Drawing Or

Use Other Visual Aids Here

The Relationship of My Dreams

For Inspiration

The late author and minister Joseph Murphy once received a letter from a widow named Ruth who had attended his lectures. She was seventy-five years old and was living on a meager income. She felt hopeless and alone. One day she chanced to remember his lecture on the power of the subconscious mind. She decided to try planting ideas in her unconscious mind. She recalled his philosophy that when purposefully and repeatedly suggesting to yourself a feeling of faith-filled expectancy, the subconscious would respond in support.

She began to saying regularly and with great feeling, *I am wanted. I am loved. I am happily married to a kind, loving, and spiritually minded man. I am secure and fulfilled.* She remarked that she did this many times each day for at least two weeks. Before too much time passed, Ruth was introduced to a retired pharmacist. He was a kind, compassionate, religious man—the answer to her prayers. Within a week's time, he asked her to marry him, and she was on her honeymoon in Europe at the time the letter was written.

Dreams of Romantic Love

Love is what dreams are made of.

—Anonymous

On the lines below, begin to write about your deepest desires for a love relationship. Be realistic and yet do not limit yourself. Be as specific as you would like. Remember, this is someone you hope to grow old with, and they will require certain qualities beyond physical characteristics or material possessions.

____

____

____

____

____

____

____

____

____

____

The Relationship of My Dreams

What philosophies do I embrace that are limiting and holding me back from pursuing my dreams?

____

____

____

____

Who could I share my dreams with for accountability and support?

____

____

____

____

What are some small steps I could take toward pursuing my dreams?

____

____

____

An affirming faith thought that can help overcome my negative and limiting beliefs is:

____

____

____

I Am Thankful For ...

Create a gratitude list on the lines below based on your awareness for a relationship or areas of contentment in your current relationship.

The Relationship of My Dreams

An Affirmation or Prayer to
Attract Your Divine Partner

The Spirit within leads us to the right person who will complete our lives and enhance our purpose. Our connection is spiritual, and divine love acts through the personality of the partner who is my perfect fit. We share love, light, peace, and joy. We bring joy to one another as we share a life full, whole, and extraordinary. I now affirm that we demonstrate being loving, spiritually connected, loyal, faithful, and truthful.

We are understanding with each other and are peaceful and loving. We are irresistibly attracted to each other. Our meeting is pure destiny, and our relationship is protected. I am building into my mind-set the type of person I dream of—a strong, powerful, successful person who will be faithful and live with integrity. Divine intelligence will bring us together in God's perfect timing.

On some level, we will recognize each other right away. I release this request to my subconscious mind and to the Creator who knows how to bring my request to pass. I am most grateful.

For Your Relationship With Your Partner

My mate and I complete each other's life and support each other's purpose. We have a spiritual union and unconditional love acts through our personalities, matching us perfectly. We share love, light, peace, and joy. I believe and feel that I am bringing joy to his/her life. We share a life full, whole, and extraordinary. I now affirm that we have these characteristics: spirituality, loyalty, faithfulness, and truth. We are patiently understanding of each other, living peacefully and lovingly toward each other. We are irresistibly attracted to each other.

Our relationship is protected, and we build into our mentality the type of people that we dream of being. We are strong, powerful, successful, faithful, and full of integrity. Our feelings are mutual and equal toward each other.

Divine intelligence knows where we are and where we are headed. Together we recognize our life's path—all in heaven's perfect timing. With gratitude, I release this request to my subconscious mind that will line up with my faith and to the Divine Spirit within me who knows how to bring my request to pass.

Modeled after prayers created by Dr. Joseph Murphy
Author of The Power of Your Subconscious Mind

Affirmations and Faith Declarations

Write your affirmations in your own prayer style or like the one above. This type of praying will build your faith as you believe for your divine partner to come into your life at just the right time and place.

Vision Page

Tape Or Glue Photos,

Magazine Cut-outs,

Sketch A Drawing Or

Use Other Visual Aids Here

Vision Page

Tape Or Glue Photos,

Magazine Cut-outs,

Sketch A Drawing Or

Use Other Visual Aids Here

The Wedding of My Dreams

For Inspiration

If you have had concerns that you will be unable to afford a nice wedding, read the following story and think again. Of course most of us know of some young couple who married with forty thousand dollars in debt due solely to their wedding and honeymoon expenses. Because of the tremendous costs of weddings, you may have concluded that your dream wedding is out of reach. I recently read an article by Bridgette Bartlette on Essence.com about a young woman who managed to have a thirty thousand dollar wedding on a six thousand dollar budget.

When asked the secret of her success, she reported several factors influencing her final wedding costs. First of all, she was very open as to what she wanted for her wedding. She didn't try to "keep up with the Joneses" and focused on what was really important—her and her husband-to-be. Secondly, she stuck to the motto of *more for less.*

This bride was not afraid or ashamed to ask people to donate their time and services to her wedding. She looked at it as a privilege to be involved in her wedding day. She was able to get a deejay at no expense by asking a friend's boyfriend. He had deejay experience but no wedding dance experience. She saw it as an opportunity for him to gain experience. The photographer she found on Craigslist.com, and he agreed to work for free in exchange for a wedding reference. A friend, a makeup artist, did her makeup in place of a wedding present. Remarkably, a friend of her husband's was a caterer and hosted their rehearsal dinner for free.

A most frugal shopper, the bride-to-be used Craigslist.com for purchases, even her wedding dress. She was able to buy a $650 dress from David's Bridal for only $200. The price tags were still attached. She bought her invitations for $30 at Party City. Another novel idea, she rented her cake from Costco where she also bought her flowers. Instead of the costly expense of wedding cake for the reception, she served sheet cake; the cake rental served only as a photo prop. The biggest expense was the location and gorgeous reception, so she opted to have the ceremony and reception in the same place.

Thus, the total cost for wedding and reception items, including the chair covers, tables, linens, and wait staff was $5,500. Conscientious of those who might not be able to afford an expensive dress, she found a dress at Delias.com on sale and was able to get free shipping. For their gifts, she went to weddingchannelstore.com and had sterling silver bracelets engraved for only eight dollars.

Even her honeymoon came at an excellent price, as the newlyweds spent over a week in the Dominican Republic enjoying an all-inclusive resort for $1500, including airfare. I believe the bride was very pleased with her wedding day and imagine that her guests were none the wiser.

My Dream Wedding

If you have not yet married, use the following worksheet to help you design your dream wedding. If you are married, you may use this section to remember your wedding and/or to visualize a ceremony in which you and your spouse retake your vows publicly.

Location:

____

Day or month preference:

____

____

Bridal wear:

____

____

Groom's attire:

____

____

Catering:

____

____

Reception:

____

____

Parties:

____

____

Shower ideas:

____

____

Wedding size or other characteristics:

____

____

Details (color scheme and décor):

____

____

Brides: (begin looking at pictures of wedding dresses online and in magazines):

____

____

____

Ethnic customs or cultural traditions:

____

____

The Wedding of My Dreams

Music:

____

____

Flowers:

____

____

Ceremony:

____

____

Honeymoon:

____

____

Gifts:

____

____

Additional notes:

____

____

____

What philosophies do I embrace that are limiting and holding me
back from pursuing my dreams?

____

____

____

Who could I share my dreams with for accountability and support?

____

____

____

What are some small steps I could take toward pursuing my dreams?

____

____

____

An affirming faith thought that can help overcome my negative and
limiting beliefs is:

____

____

____

____

The Wedding of My Dreams

I Am Thankful For ...

On the lines below, write what you can be grateful for in retrospect about your wedding or others you were involved in, and those good experiences that may influence your own wedding.

Affirmations and Faith Declarations

My wedding plans are divinely guided, and I have the wedding of my dreams.

Using the above affirmation as an example, write your own affirmations or faith declarations about your current desires for your wedding as if they were already met.

The Wedding of My Dreams

Vision Page

Tape Or Glue Photos,

Magazine Cut-outs,

Sketch A Drawing Or

Use Other Visual Aids Here

Vision Page

Tape Or Glue Photos,

Magazine Cut-outs,

Sketch A Drawing Or

Use Other Visual Aids Here

Vision Page

Tape Or Glue Photos,

Magazine Cut-outs,

Sketch A Drawing Or

Use Other Visual Aids Here

Vision Page

Tape Or Glue Photos,

Magazine Cut-outs,

Sketch A Drawing Or

Use Other Visual Aids Here

My Dreams
of Family

For Inspiration

By the age of forty-two, Julia Indichova had an FSH level of 42 and was told her chances of conceiving were few to none. There were no documented cases of anyone conceiving a child with an FSH of 42. Julia then began what she refers to in her book, *Inconceivable,* as the "fertility roller coaster." She followed a self-prescribed treatment that consisted of a lifestyle change and alternative treatments, including major diet modifications and taking herbs.

After eight months had passed, Julia made an appointment with a very expensive specialist as a last-ditch effort only to find out she was already pregnant. She gave birth to her daughter nine months later. Julia writes, "Though I was unaware of it at the time, this journey was more about learning to believe in myself than about getting pregnant. It was the first time in my life I dared to follow through on all the healthy impulses that urged me to keep going."

After this amazing journey, a dream was birthed in Julia's heart to share her experience of struggle and triumph with the world. Thirteen years later, she is a famous author and founder of the webzine FertileHeart.com. She runs ongoing support groups and workshops in New York City and Woodstock. She also travels around the country speaking about fertility and health empowerment. Her life is a reminder to never underestimate the power of your dreams.

My Dream Family

If you hope to have children either now or in the future, journal about the dreams you have for your family. If you are a parent, envision your children's dreams and the relationship you hope to maintain throughout their lives. If you've passed the age for parenting, write about your dreams for your extended family or social network. You may have hopes for improved connection or better communication with them.

____

____

____

____

____

____

____

____

____

> It can be frightening; this yearning for a child—it's hard to fathom the desperate urgency.
> —Wendy Wasserstein, from *Creating a Life* by Sylvia Hewett, as quoted in *The Infertility Cure.*

What philosophies do I embrace that are limiting and holding me back from pursuing my dreams?

____

____

____

Who could I share my dreams with for accountability and support?

____

____

____

What are some small steps I could take toward pursuing my dreams?

____

____

An affirming faith thought that can help overcome my negative and limiting beliefs is:

____

____

____

____

I Am Thankful For ...

On the lines below, write any blessings you experience from your family relationships. Search to see if there is any unforgiveness blocking your relationships from being the soul connections they really could become.

Affirmations and Faith Declarations

I solve all of the problems facing me concerning family issues
by placing my complete trust in the mystery of the Creator and
Divine power that lives within me.

Using the above affirmation as an example, write your own affirmations or faith declarations about your current dreams or future
desires for your family.

____

____

____

____

____

____

____

____

____

____

____

____

Vision Page

Tape Or Glue Photos,

Magazine Cut-outs,

Sketch A Drawing Or

Use Other Visual Aids Here

My Dreams of Family

Vision Page

Tape Or Glue Photos,

Magazine Cut-outs,

Sketch A Drawing Or

Use Other Visual Aids Here

Vegas **Cancun** *Hawaii* **Ixtapa** *Mazatlan* **Paris** Vienna **San Francisco** *New Orleans* Lake Tahoe **Santa Fe** *Houston* **Orlando Heidelberg Morocco Italy Calgary** The Florida Keys **Jamaica** *Istanbul* **Costa Rica Mexico** *Roswell* Venice **Eiffel Tower** *Leaning Tower Of Piza* **Greece Israel** *Reno* **Baja Caribbean Ft. Lauder**dale Antigua Niagara Falls Anguilla Scotland Rome *Florence* Italy Tuscany *Luxembourg* Fiji Islands Belize China Argentina Nevada City, Ca **Branson, Mo** *Myrtle Beach* **San Diego, Ca** New York City Vermont France Yellowstone Hungary Portugal Spain United Kingdom *Venezuela* Finland **India San Antonio**, Texas Alaska Puerto Rico Williamsburg, Virginia **Colorado** Sedona, Arizona *Galveston* The Great Lakes Utah South **Padre Island** Biloxi **Atlantic City** Wyoming Turner Falls, Ok Washington *Philadelphia* Vancouver *Switzerland* Ireland Sardinia Cayman Islands Provence, France **Turner Falls** Mexico City Guatemala **Australia** New Zealand Bali *Washington, D.C.* Tofiono, British Columbia Bulgaria Miami, Florida **Memphis, Tennesee** *Mount Rushmore* **Atlinburg** Prague Barcelona Amsterdam Milan Munich Tahiti **Bermuda Trench Coat** *Africa* **Egypt** Brazil **Cruise** Bed-and-breakfast **Los Angeles** Boston *Atlanta* **Big Sur British Virgin Islands Rio De Janeiro, Brazil Thailand**

My Vacation Dreams

My Vacation Dreams

For Inspiration

In *Making Your Dreams Come True*, Marcia Wieder writes about how she created a project she called "Go On at Least One Free and Fun Cruise to an Exotic Place Within the Next Three Months." She then listed ways she could achieve this dream. Since part of her project included the cruise being free, she couldn't list purchasing a ticket as part of her strategy. She decided that a bartering relationship would be one way.

She focused her energy on a particular cruise line, and her goal was to have a workshop booked on their cruise ship in exchange for a free trip. She took action, sending out a promotional package to her cruise line of choice. Before she even made a follow-up call to see if they were interested in her package, they called her to confirm. The free cruise in exchange for her workshop was booked about five months ahead of what she had even hoped for herself.

> Let's dream and imagine and be practical strategists. Let's dream and make our dreams come true.
>
> —Marcia Wieder

My Dreams of Travel

Using the previous *idea* page, identify your dream vacation destinations on the lines provided below. Expound on what your specific visions are for places, types of tours, and interesting activities.

What philosophies do I embrace that are limiting and holding me
back from pursuing my dreams?

____

____

____

Who could I share my dreams with for accountability and support?

____

____

____

What are some small steps I could take toward pursuing my dreams?

____

____

____

An affirming faith thought that can help overcome my negative and
limiting beliefs is:

____

____

____

I Am Thankful For...

On the lines below, write about vacations taken or future plans that you can be grateful for today. Reminisce about places you've been in the past.

Declarations

Opportunities for travel present themselves to me just when I need them the most and in a manner which is affordable and comfortable.

Using the above affirmation as an example, write your own affirmations or faith declarations about your dreams for travel.

____

____

____

____

____

____

____

____

____

____

____

Vision Page

Tape Or Glue Photos,

Magazine Cut-outs,

Sketch A Drawing Or

Use Other Visual Aids Here

Vision Page

Tape Or Glue Photos,

Magazine Cut-outs,

Sketch A Drawing Or

Use Other Visual Aids Here

KNITTING Sewing *Needlepoint* Quilting **Crochet** Bird Watching Painting Sketch Artist **saltwater aquarium** POKER **BOATING** motorcycles *MOUNTAINCLIMBING* ballroom dancing *SHOPPING* sight-seeing INVESTING **COLLECTIBLES** *WOODWORKING* model planes FOREIGN LANGUAGE **vintage wear** CRAFTS *Electronics* Trains Kites Sculpting Gaming Home Renovation Racing Dinosaurs **Crossword** Puzzles *Renaissance* Fair Paper Mache Machine **Work** Baking Wedding CAKES gardening *Volunteer* WORK rockets **MODEL** TRAINS ANTIQUES COIN COLLECTING blogging swimming fashion design *GOLFING* TENNIS **POOL** POKER ANTIQUE BOOKS SKY DIVING Inventing Costumes **Make-overs** Hair Nail Art Tattoos Self-help Scrapbooking Cartooning Raw Foods Gourmet Cooking Boating SKIING FINE-LOOKING **myspace** SKATING art galleries MUSIC POSTERS herb **gardening** ANCIENT **CASTLES** chess *FISHING* Facebook Gourmet *Coffee* Alternative Remedies Writing Pets Watches Clocks **Poetry** Deep-sea Fishing Furniture Restoral *Photography* ARCHAEOLOGY Rodeo Landscape Masonery Acting Musicals Comedy *Jewelry* **Making Braids** Musical **Instruments** worship services AMUSEMENT PARKS

                                   My Hobbies

My Hobbies

For Inspiration

How I Became an Artist

Many people have a casual attitude toward art, and I was no exception. I was born in 1948 and raised in the fifties on a poor ranch in Texas. I hardly knew what a city was, much less anything about art or being an artist. In the early sixties, my parents divorced, and we moved to a tiny Texas town that boasted of one grocery store, a gas station, and a high school with a class of ten students total.

Art was never even a passing thought as I continued my walk in life, getting married, having children, working, getting divorced twice, and all that goes with the struggle to survive more obstacles than I will take time to discuss during this writing. Dreams did not find a place in my thoughts very often in those days, and if I did allow a dream to flicker across my mind, I would not dwell on it for very long.

In the year of 1989, I was finally beginning to realize that life might have something more to offer. The man of my dreams, my third husband, Ray, had asked me to retire six months earlier. During that time, I somehow began watching an oil painting show on TV, "The Joy of Painting," with Bob Ross. I was fascinated. It was not very long before I really wanted to try and paint along with this man on TV. Ray was excited I was interested in painting, and he encouraged me to the highest degree. He began video taping art programs.

One weekend he took me shopping for paints, brushes, canvas, and any items I would need to paint. Our apartment was very small, and we set everything up on the dining room table so I could paint with the video. My first finished painting was a landscape. Everyone praised my work and encouraged me to continue. Painting became my absolute passion in life. I would paint from early in the morning until my husband would get home from work. A dream was birthed in the depths of my soul.

A few months later, we started looking to buy a four-bedroom house. We had prayed and asked God to lead, direct, and guide us to just the right home to purchase. The one we found and really loved had brand-new, lush, thick carpet in all the rooms except one small bedroom in the back corner. This room had old, stained carpet, and needed repairs. I knew God had chosen this room to become my very own, and when the renovations were complete, it was the perfect art studio. We began buying art how-to books, videos, and all the supplies I would possibly need. I painted constantly, almost day and night. I would often finish two paintings per day!

About a year later, we began attending a little church in our neighborhood. We became friends with the young pastor and his family. When they found out that I was an artist, they asked me to teach their sons how to paint. They had two adorable little boys that were homeschooled, and it was not long before I began teaching the boys to paint once per week in my studio. When contemplating whether or not to charge for the lessons, I remembered a verse from the Bible that says, "Freely I have received, and freely I give" (Matthew 10:8, NIV). I believed that God had given me the gift of painting, so I did not charge any money for the art lessons, and we provided all the supplies needed, except the canvas for the lessons.

The next five and a half years were filled with students from ages six to seventy coming in and out of my studio twice per week and learning how to paint. At one time, I had eighteen students per week.

This was a great time of learning and growing for me as an artist. There was an unending wealth of artistic knowledge to absorb. I was like a sponge and wanted to learn more. After I stopped teaching, my interest moved from painting landscapes toward painting people. This was very foreign to me because I had never studied how to draw much. Ray discovered different ways to place a picture onto canvas without drawing it, so we bought a projector. This method worked very well for several years and was later replaced by enlarging items on the computer. I would trace the picture onto a canvas using graphite paper.

During these years, I sold paintings, accepted commissions for specific works, and did *plein air* paintings in public occasionally (*Plein air* painters work at a particular outside location, capturing the light effects that occur in nature). The majority of my paintings were given to family members and just about anyone who wanted them.

Many times, I would get very frustrated with a painting and throw it out to the curb for trash pick up. Ray would retrieve some of them and hide them in the attic. Many times, after months had gone by, he would bring a painting down, and I would wonder why I had thrown it away! A neighbor invited me into her home one day and sheepishly admitted she had taken some of my paintings from our trash and placed them on her walls.

Ray had also developed a great interest in learning to paint. We took a spring vacation near a beautiful, large lake in Texas and decided we would paint together for a week. After the first day of painting, I became very ill and thought it was a stomach virus or something I had eaten. In fact, I had been having stomach problems for a few weeks prior. When we arrived back home, we decided to clean the studio really well and bought a powerful air refresher device for the room, because my husband had noticed that almost every time I painted, I became very ill at my stomach. After some research, we realized I had developed a strong allergy to oil paints and turpentine! We got rid of any and all oil-based products in the studio and started over using a water-based acrylic paint. It was quite expensive.

Learning to paint with acrylics presented a huge challenge, as they dry quickly in a matter of seconds and are nearly impossible to blend in comparison to oil paints, which take several days to dry completely, and blending is no problem at all. Lots of new videos were studied, and I continued to paint every day, determined to learn the new medium. One weekend, I decided to paint a twenty-four-by-thirty-six-inch canvas and chose a landscape composition with an old chapel high up in the mountains. I was painting as fast as I possibly could before the acrylic dried, and Ray laughingly said I was painting with both hands! When that experience was complete, I knew I could paint anything I wanted with acrylics.

The old master painters from the sixteenth through eighteenth centuries are fascinating, and I learned as much as possible about their lives. My favorites are John William Waterhouse, Renoir, Dante Gabriel Rosetti, Sir Frank Dicksee, Pierre Auguste Cot, and far too many others to name.

Thus began my love affair with these exceptional, talented, brilliant, and extraordinary master artists who simply referred to themselves as *painters*. I began painting my own renditions of their beautiful compositions to hang on the walls of our home. The two largest size canvases I have painted are thirty-six by forty-eight inches. We found a fabulous wholesale company and bought the most exquisite and superb frames we could afford.

A few years later, we moved into a beautiful new home closer to our family. We renovated an extra bedroom into a studio to comfortably accommodate our easels, chairs, storage cabinet, tables, and all our art supplies. Eventually, we joined a local art association that met once per month, and we enjoyed making new friendships with other artists. We exhibited in art shows, banks, and various other places during our tenure with the group.

In November of 2005, I became president of my own art association, which was formed with the help of some very close and dear artist friends. We were a diverse group of lively, creative, and energetic artists that met once per month in a local chamber of commerce. Our meetings were fun, boisterous, and informative. We always encouraged one another to keep painting, no matter what! We exhibited paintings in different businesses on a continual basis, and our artwork remains displayed at the city library to this day. The association was disbanded in December 2008. Many lifelong friendships were developed during this time in my life, and I will forever be grateful for this special experience.

Through these years of painting, there have been many lessons I learned and continue to learn about the importance of reaching toward ones dreams; knowing the Master Creator, God, has shared some of his very own abilities to create beautiful works of art through my existence on this earth. Each time I complete an outstanding and exceptional painting, I feel like I have just awakened a place deep within my soul, discovering a river of abundant, overflowing life filled with delight.

Printed by permission from Janice "Celeste" Hunt of Celeste Arts, Saginaw, TX

My Hobbies

My Hobbies

Hobbies I'd Like to Have One Day

In this busy world, *hobby* isn't even a word we hear used very often. Exploring the most popular hobbies people take pleasure in can lead to enjoyable and fulfilling rewards in your life. According to buzzle. com, psychologists have this to say: "Having certain preoccupations (hobbies) makes your life quality grow by enhancing the level of happiness." We humans seem to derive a strong sense of fulfillment from having successfully accomplished certain tasks. This sense of fulfillment does amazing things for us both mentally and physically. So what exactly is a hobby? Here is one definition:

> a certain activity or process that gives people the opportunity to tap into their creative side, following the inspiration that creative energy brings into the accomplishment of a certain project.

Using the many hobbies listed on the previous page, list below those that appeal to you, sound fun and rewarding. Expound a bit on what might be enjoyable about that particular hobby and ways you could get started. If you already have a hobby, write about the dreams you may have ignored or been procrastinating to pursue.

What philosophies do I embrace that are limiting and holding me back from pursuing my dreams?

____

____

____

Who could I share my dreams with for accountability and support?

____

____

My Hobbies

What are some small steps I could take toward pursuing my dreams?

____

____

____

An affirming faith thought that can help overcome my negative and limiting beliefs is:

____

____

____

I am Thankful For ...

Make a gratitude list of pastimes you currently enjoy that help you lead a full life.

____

____

____

____

____

____

____

Affirmations and Faith Declarations

My creativity flows when I am working with my talents and abilities through my hobbies. I am in touch with my creative genius and celebrate my accomplishments.

On the lines below, create your own affirmations based on the dreams you have for your creative outlets.

____

____

____

____

____

____

____

____

____

____

Vision Page

Tape Or Glue Photos,

Magazine Cut-outs,

Sketch A Drawing Or

Use Other Visual Aids Here

Vision Page

Tape Or Glue Photos,

Magazine Cut-outs,

Sketch A Drawing Or

Use Other Visual Aids Here

Vision Page

Tape Or Glue Photos,

Magazine Cut-outs,

Sketch A Drawing Or

Use Other Visual Aids Here

Subjects I Want to Learn About

For Inspiration

Asking For What You Want in Support of Your Dreams

During a career change in my early thirties, I realized I needed to learn Spanish so I could work with Spanish-speaking people. I studied with software programs and tapes that friends had let me borrow, and I bought a few books. My progress was okay, but I wasn't speaking Spanish, and I certainly did not understand those persons at work speaking Spanish.

Then one day it occurred to me. What I really needed was a friend who didn't speak English so that I had the opportunity to actually communicate in Spanish. I didn't know any Spanish-speaking people who didn't speak English at the time. I encountered them at the store and so forth, but either I didn't meet them in a social context, or they spoke English which I knew would never work because we would invariably end up speaking English.

So I prayed and asked for someone to come into my life that only spoke Spanish. I purposefully tried to believe it would be possible somehow and felt expectant for an answered prayer.

One day, I noticed two women moving up on the third floor. I heard them speaking Spanish, but I thought it might be because they didn't have any English-speaking friends with them. Later, I noticed that they never spoke English. They were about my age, looked friendly, and so eventually I got up the nerve to say *hola*. There are no words to describe how nervous I was, and yet the barrier was broken and a relationship began.

To make a long story short, I eventually became roommates and shared an apartment with those Spanish-speaking neighbors for several years. After they moved back to Mexico, I went to visit them several times. Imagine how much that experience improved my Spanish; in fact, it changed my life forever.

I eventually was hired to teach bilingual third grade, passed the teacher's state certification exam in Spanish, and taught high school Spanish I and II. Studying Spanish is a hobby and passion of mine to this day! I've thoroughly enjoyed my experiences and relationships with people from places like Mexico, Cuba, Guatemala, and Puerto Rico, to name a few.

I've learned that a dream can be anything you desire to have or achieve that blesses you and others. In addition to attaining money, fame, or success, a dream is also experiencing a rich, fulfilling life in areas of heart and home.

Subjects I Want to Learn

What I'd Like to Learn

You see things; and you say, "Why?" But I dream things that never were; and I say, "Why not?"
—George Bernard Shaw

What philosophies do I embrace that are limiting and holding me back from pursuing my dreams?

____

____

____

Who could I share my dreams with for accountability and support?

____

____

____

What are some small steps I could take toward pursuing my dreams?

____

____

____

An affirming faith thought that can help overcome my negative and limiting beliefs is:

____

____

I Am Thankful For ...

On the lines below, write about subjects you've studied in the past or special interests you have you are looking forward to learning about.

Subjects I Want to Learn

Affirmations or Faith Declaration

I can succeed. All that is possible to anyone is possible to me.
I AM successful. I do succeed, for I am full of the Power of
Success.

—Wallace D. Wattles

Using the above affirmation as an example, write your own declarations about subject matter you intend to learn.

____

____

____

____

____

____

____

____

____

____

____

____

Vision Page

Tape Or Glue Photos,

Magazine Cut-outs,

Sketch A Drawing Or

Use Other Visual Aids Here

Vision Page

Tape Or Glue Photos,

Magazine Cut-outs,

Sketch A Drawing Or

Use Other Visual Aids Here

Things I Want to Own Some Day

For Inspiration

In *The Power of Your Subconscious Mind,* by the late Dr. Joseph Murphy, he writes about a young woman who personally told him of an incredible experience of hers. Nina was a college student and was only browsing through the ritzy shopping areas of Beverly Hills, when she passed a beautiful leather bag that really appealed to her. She checked the price tag only to gasp and think to herself that she could never afford an accessory that expensive. Immediately she caught her negative thinking because of Dr. Murphy's teaching: *never finish a negative statement.* She then made a different statement to herself affirming that the handbag was for sale, and she would one day receive that bag for her very own.

The young lady was engaged at the time and was meeting her fiancé for dinner. The couple was to be parted for a few days and when her husband-to-be arrived, he was carrying a nicely wrapped gift under his arm. With great anticipation, she removed the wrappings of the present only to discover it was the same red shoulder bag she had eyed earlier while shopping.

My Dreams of Having Things

There are probably many things you could list right off the top of your head that you would like to own. Write those things on the lines below, as well as possessions you could own that would be a blessing to others.

What philosophies do I embrace that are limiting and holding me
back from pursuing my dreams?

____

____

____

Who could I share my dreams with for accountability and support?

____

____

____

What are some small steps I could take toward pursuing my dreams?

____

____

____

An affirming faith thought that can help overcome my negative and
limiting beliefs is:

____

____

____

____

I Am Thankful For ...

On the lines below, create a list of your possessions that you may take for granted but for which you are really grateful to own. Include things that make your life easier, more pleasant, or meaningful in some way.

____

____

____

____

____

____

____

____

____

____

____

____

____

Things I Want to Own

Affirmations or Faith Declaration

Everything I need comes to me. I am blessed in all ways with an abundant lifestyle.

Using the above affirmation as an example, write your own declarations about subject matter you intend to learn.

____

____

____

____

____

____

____

____

____

____

____

____

Vision Page

Tape Or Glue Photos,

Magazine Cut-outs,

Sketch A Drawing Or

Use Other Visual Aids Here

Vision Page

Tape Or Glue Photos,

Magazine Cut-outs,

Sketch A Drawing Or

Use Other Visual Aids Here

Vision Page

Tape Or Glue Photos,

Magazine Cut-outs,

Sketch A Drawing Or

Use Other Visual Aids Here

Things I Want to Own

My Dreams of Community

Involvement and Philanthropy

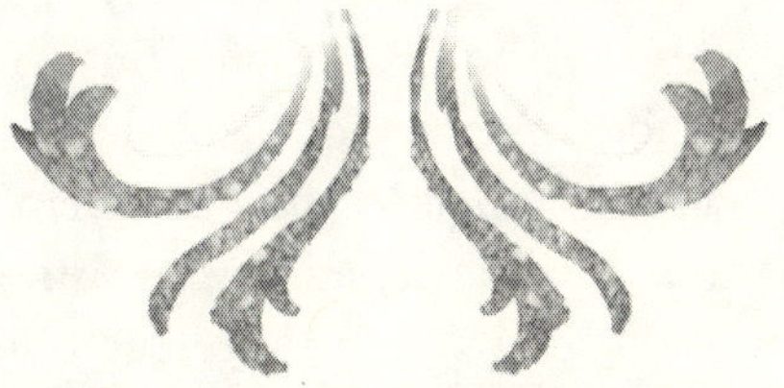

I absolutely believe in the power of tithing and giving back. My own experience about all the blessings I've had in my life is that the more I give away, the more that comes back. That is the way life works, and that is the way energy works.

—Ken Blanchard

For Inspiration

You may think of philanthropy as something only available to the rich. If you have a desire to make a positive difference, however, you can do this without being rich or famous. Perhaps it seems that volunteer work with your current schedule is out of the question. At Everydaygiving.com, Roger Carr and his organization are encouraging people from all walks of life to become what he refers to as an "Everyday Philanthropist." Carr writes, "You don't have to be rich, famous, or retired to make a difference in the world every day!" The Web site offers a free special report, *9 Questions to Consider Before Volunteering,* to help his readers recognize the volunteer opportunity that is the best fit for them. Referred to as a "Mentor to the Rich of Heart," Mr. Carr and his Web site offer free information to help others make their dreams of giving come true. Barbara Bush has said that "some people give time, some money, some their skills and connections, some literally give their life's blood. But everyone has something to give."

The word "philanthropy" actually stems from an Ancient Greek word that means *to love people*. We tend to think of philanthropists as wealthy people, and many of them are, in fact, quite rich. But a philanthropist doesn't have to possess great wealth. They are people who donate time, services, supplies, and money to support beneficial organizations or improve the quality of human life. They do not expect anything tangible in return for their donations.

On the lines below, dream about humanitarian causes or charity organizations that you imagine donating your time or money to support. You may want to spend some time researching on the internet the common areas in which people volunteer to include the fine arts, performing arts, educational institutions, or religious organizations that support ministry or worldwide needs.

Organizations that interest me:

____

____

____

Causes that move me:

____

____

____

My Dreams of Community

My dreams for a better community, town, city, country, and world:

____

Social injustices that alarm me:

____

____

____

____

____

____

____

____

____

____

____

What philosophies do I embrace that are limiting and holding me back from pursuing my dreams?

____

____

____

Who could I share my dreams with for accountability and support?

____

____

____

What are some small steps I could take toward pursuing my dreams?

____

____

____

An affirming faith thought that can help overcome my negative and limiting beliefs is:

____

____

____

My Dreams of Community

I Am Thankful For ...

Journal about individuals or organizations for which you are grateful—those that have touched you, inspired you, or helped you in any way.

Affirmations or Faith Declaration

I am blessed in every area of my life with wealth. I am a generous person with many opportunities to bless others, and the more I give away, the more I receive in blessings returned.

Using the above affirmation as an example, write your own declarations about subject matter you intend to learn.

____

____

____

____

____

____

____

____

____

____

____

____

My Dreams of Community

Vision Page

Tape Or Glue Photos,

Magazine Cut-outs,

Sketch A Drawing Or

Use Other Visual Aids Here

Vision Page

Tape Or Glue Photos,

Magazine Cut-outs,

Sketch A Drawing Or

Use Other Visual Aids Here

My Spiritual Aspirations

Dreams pass into the reality of action. From the actions stems the dream again; and this interdependence produces the highest form of living.

—Anais Nin

To accomplish great things, we must not only act, but also dream, not only plan, but also believe.

—Anatole France

And when you assume the posture of prayer, remember that it's not all asking. If you have anything against someone, forgive, only then will your heavenly Father be included to also wipe your slate clean.

Mark 11:24 (The Message Bible)

For Inspiration

About five years ago, I read a book about a near-death incident a man from my home state experienced. The book was intriguing, reaffirming my beliefs in a Creator and the supernatural. Being from Texas, I was even familiar with the area in which his accident took place. While his account of a near-death experience was captivating, the account of his recovery was just as absorbing.

I pray that Don Piper's experience will inspire you to explore your own spiritual beliefs and help you move toward your dreams of spiritual connection with a divine power greater than yourself.

My Spiritual Aspirations

On January 18, 1989, Don Piper was killed instantly in a tragic car wreck. Paramedics who arrived quickly on the scene found no pulse and therefore pronounced him dead. Covered by a tarp to hide his tangled mess of flesh, he was unaware of what had happened to him or anyone around him. One minute he was alive on earth and the next he recalls being in a different dimension that he refers to as *heaven*.

A Baptist preacher named Dick Onerecker was driving with his wife along the same highway where Don's accident took place. Since traffic was brought to a complete halt, and being a minister, he and his wife walked to see if they could be of help or comfort to anyone. The EMTs told him everyone was okay, but the man in the red car, Don, was dead. Strangely, Dick felt strongly he needed to pray for Don. The EMTs scoffed at Dick, but upon his insistence, told him to do whatever he felt he needed to do.

So he prayed fervently like he'd never prayed before. Certainly praying in this sort of situation went entirely against his theology, but he felt so strongly God had told him to do it that he felt he had no choice.

About ninety minutes after the man in the red car was pronounced dead, the prayers of the preacher were answered. Although reluctantly, Don Piper did return to his badly broken earthly body, never to be the same again.

Summary from the prologue of *90 Minutes in Heaven* by Don Piper

My Dreams of Spiritual Growth

On the lines below, write about the spiritual growth you desire, areas
of your life that you hope to improve and seek positive change.

What fears do I feel about my dreams?

____

____

____

____

What philosophies do I embrace that are limiting and holding me
back from pursuing my dreams?

____

____

____

____

Who could I share my dreams with for accountability and support?

____

____

____

What are some small steps I could take toward pursuing my dreams?

____

____

____

____

I Am Thankful For ...

On the lines below, create a list of spiritual blessings for which you are thankful.

Affirmations or Faith Declaration

Blessed *be* the God and Father of our Lord Jesus Christ, who
has blessed us with every spiritual blessing in the heavenly *places*
in Christ...

Ephesians 1:3 (NKJV)

On the lines below, write your own affirmations using sacred pas-
sages or faith-thoughts about your relationship with the Creator.
First Person, by Ray Hunt, is an excellent resource for praying using
Scripture in a personally affirming, faith-building manner.

____

____

____

____

____

____

____

____

____

____

Vision Page

Tape Or Glue Photos,

Magazine Cut-outs,

Sketch A Drawing Or

Use Other Visual Aids Here

My Retirement Dreams

You are what you think about all day long.
—Dr. Robert Schuller

For Inspiration

After thirty-six years of teaching at Texas A&M and a very successful career in his preferred field of interest, my daughter's grandfather, Richard Frederiksen, alongside his lovely wife, Phyllis, retired and moved their residence out of state. When looking for someone to inspire my retirement dreams, I did not have to look far. This couple continues to be a source of inspiration for those who know them.

Partly due to health reasons and partially to follow a dream, they decided to move to Albuquerque, New Mexico. After so many years of living in the same community with deep roots, they dared displace themselves. Making such an enormous change upon retirement and leaving their deep friendships and community involvement must have been challenging. Leaving so many connections behind and the familiarities of a well-established home could lead to feelings of disillusionment. They chose to brave those challenges by pursuing their passions, interests, and new friendships.

Through efforts to establish church membership, community involvement, and continued professional interests and travel, they created what appears to be the life of their dreams. Joining breakfast groups and working the voting polls, they supported their political beliefs through various resources. With the freedom to set their own schedules, they took tours like the "Smithsonian Tour of the Spoleto Festival" and began singing with the University Chorus, to name a few activities.

Becoming involved with organizations like the Albuquerque Museum Foundation, they are always in the *know* about available, interesting exhibits. Working with programs like University Showcase, at a local radio station, keeps Papa informed and connected as well as utilizes his talents and expertise. They have met some wonderfully interesting people and formed new friendships. Having followed the forces that drew them to the area, they discovered the beauty and rich cultural background New Mexico offers. Ultimately they reaped far more than just physical benefits.

In addition to these activities, they are health conscious and incorporate both a healthy diet and exercise into their lifestyle. They have maintained strong family connections through emails, letters, birthday and holiday celebrations, and phone calls. Even though they live out of state, they are visited often by friends and family. Because of their awareness of their city and state, we have experienced some wonderful sightseeing when we visit. Whether it was hiking on Sandia or visiting the ancient home of the cliff dwellers, they were never lacking for recreational ideas.

Certainly one of their secrets to a winning retirement was being financially prepared. Another key to their success has been their continued interest in learning. Whether they were at home or abroad with a local tour group, they found educational opportunities like attending lectures while traveling.

Over the years I have received emails and photos from this couple humorously bragging about the weather and wonderful views of Sandia from their backyard. I love to see Phyllis's face light up when she talks about living there. When I think about this couple in retirement, I am truly inspired to lead a fuller, more rewarding lifestyle both now and in the future. Naturally, I am inspired to dream, imagining my retirement to be very much like theirs.

Retirement can be the most enjoyable time of your life with careful thought, planning, and a flexibility to try new things. Some people return to school and study long-held interests they were unable to pursue while working and/or raising a family.

Financial planning for retirement can be started at any age and should be started as soon as possible. Most young people don't realize that by starting to save early, letting those savings accrue interest, they can have a large sum of money by the time they reach retirement age. Having money for retirement is a wonderful and important thing. Some may think of the retired as old people sitting in rocking chairs, whittling on sticks, and spitting snuff. Not today's retirees!

They are involved in their community, politics, volunteer opportunities, and belong to senior citizen organizations. Some turn their hobbies into income-making adventures, involve themselves with family, and have the time to pursue their unfulfilled dreams. When it comes to retirement, it is time to think outside the box.

Dreams for My Retirement

Retirement gives you the time to fulfill lifetime dreams. It's like reverting back to a childhood of play, joy, and discovery.
—Sharon Anne Waldrop with Bankrate.com

On the lines below, write the first thing that comes to mind about your dream retirement. You may list how much money you would like to save, things you look forward to doing in retirement that you don't have time to do now.

My Retirement Dreams

What fears do I feel about my dreams?

____

____

____

What philosophies do I embrace that are limiting and holding me back from pursuing my dreams?

____

____

____

____

Who could I share my dreams with for accountability and support?

____

____

____

What are some small steps I could take toward pursuing my dreams?

____

____

____

____

An affirming faith thought or affirmation that can help overcome my negative and limiting beliefs is:

____

____

____

I Am Thankful For ...

On the lines below, list knowledge or insights you've gained or retirement plans for which you can feel grateful. Write about any-thing or anyone in relation to this subject that brings up thoughts of gratitude.

____

____

____

____

____

____

____

____

My Retirement Dreams

Affirmations and Faith Declarations

I make exciting retirements plans. I plant thoughts of a rewarding retirement into my subconscious and know that God is faithful, rewarding me for my good labor, and my plans shall come to pass.

Using the above affirmation as an example, write your own affirmations or faith declarations according to your retirement dreams.

____

____

____

____

____

____

____

____

____

____

____

____

Vision Page

Vision Page

Tape Or Glue Photos,

Magazine Cut-outs,

Sketch A Drawing Or

Use Other Visual Aids Here

Vision Page

Tape Or Glue Photos,

Magazine Cut-outs,

Sketch A Drawing Or

Use Other Visual Aids Here

In My Golden Years

Regardless of what supplements you take and what kind of exercise you do, when all is said and done, it is your attitude, your beliefs, and your daily thought patterns that have the most profound effect on your health.
 —Christiane Northrup, M.D., *The Wisdom of Menopause*

For Inspiration

In the fall of 1914, Jack LaLanne was born in San Francisco, California. His childhood years were spent eating the standard American diet, but at age fifteen he heard health pioneer Paul Bragg speak about nutrition and health. Bragg's speech made a deep impression on the young LaLanne, and he improved his nutrition and began to study bodybuilding, chiropractic medicine, and weightlifting. None of these areas of health were popular in the 1930's. The first fitness authority to promote women lifting weights, Jack broke through gender and other barriers in health-related fitness. By the 1980s there were more than two hundred Jack LaLanne health clubs. These clubs were eventually sold and are now known as Bally's Total Fitness.

Jack is a person who pursued his passion and his dreams. When his TV show was first aired, his critics said it wouldn't last past six weeks. Jack, however, was on the air just a little over thirty-four years. Jack is now in his mid-nineties and still works out about an hour-and-a-half a day in addition to his cardiovascular workout.

Dreams for Your Golden Years

When you are young, conscious thoughts that you will one day have an aged body don't occur too often. But as any senior citizen will tell you, it happens quicker than one expects. Take a few moments now and think about your goals for your life when in your late 70's, 80's or even 90's.

What are your health goals? Where would you like to live when you're ninety years old? While it may seem those years are in the very distant future, the truth is, the lifestyle you lead now will determine the lifestyle you'll have then. Start dreaming about the winter years of your life on the lines below. No one *wants* to get old, but you have to admit—it's better than the alternative.

____

____

____

____

____

____

____

____

____

What fears do I feel about my dreams?

____

____

____

____

What philosophies do I embrace that are limiting and holding me
back from pursuing my dreams?

____

____

____

____

Who could I share my dreams with for accountability and support?

____

____

____

____

What are some small steps I could take toward pursuing my dreams?

____

____

____

____

An affirming faith thought or affirmation that can help overcome
my negative and limiting beliefs is:

____

____

____

I Am Thankful For ...

On the lines below, write a gratitude list concerning your life or
important senior citizens in your life.

____

____

____

____

____

____

____

____

____

Affirmations and Faith Declarations

My Lord has carried me from the day I was born; And will keep
on carrying me when I'm old … bearing me when I'm old and
gray … saving me.

Isaiah 46:3–4, MSG

Using the above paraphrase from an Old Testament scripture as an
example, write your own faith declarations about your golden years.

____

____

____

____

____

____

____

____

____

____

____

____

Vision Page

Tape Or Glue Photos,

Magazine Cut-outs,

Sketch A Drawing Or

Use Other Visual Aids Here

Vision Page

Tape Or Glue Photos,

Magazine Cut-outs,

Sketch A Drawing Or

Use Other Visual Aids Here

Vision Page

Tape Or Glue Photos,

Magazine Cut-outs,

Sketch A Drawing Or

Use Other Visual Aids Here

My List of
Dreams Come True

As time goes by, you will find more and more of the dreams written in these pages being realized. Take the time to review your *journal* and jot down your accomplishments both great and small. This is an important activity, as remembering your fulfilled dreams builds your hope and faith in a Divine Power greater than yourself. Use this as a source of encouragement to persevere if certain events do not occur when you had wanted. Add photographs taken during these times to the following *Vision Pages*.

____

____

____

____

____

____

Vision Page

Tape Or Glue Photos,

Magazine Cut-outs,

Sketch A Drawing Or

Use Other Visual Aids Here

Vision Page

Tape Or Glue Photos,

Magazine Cut-outs,

Sketch A Drawing Or

Use Other Visual Aids Here

Vision Page

Tape Or Glue Photos,

Magazine Cut-outs,

Sketch A Drawing Or

Use Other Visual Aids Here

Dreams Come True

Vision Page

Tape Or Glue Photos,

Magazine Cut-outs,

Sketch A Drawing Or

Use Other Visual Aids Here

Vision Page

Tape Or Glue Photos,

Magazine Cut-outs,

Sketch A Drawing Or

Use Other Visual Aids Here

Vision Page

Tape Or Glue Photos,

Magazine Cut-outs,

Sketch A Drawing Or

Use Other Visual Aids Here

Vision Page

Tape Or Glue Photos,

Magazine Cut-outs,

Sketch A Drawing Or

Use Other Visual Aids Here

Dreams Come True

Vision Page

Tape Or Glue Photos,

Magazine Cut-outs,

Sketch A Drawing Or

Use Other Visual Aids Here

Notes about My Journey

Gore Vidal, in his memoir Palimpsest, gave a personal definition of the word memoir: "A memoir is how one remembers one's own life, while an autobiography is history, requiring research, dates, facts double-checked."

Important Life Lessons I've Learned Along the Way

Use this section as a place for your memoir. Write about what you have gleaned from pursuing your dreams rather than about the outcome of your life as a whole.

____

____

____

____

____

Notes

Notes

Suggested Reading List

The Finish Rich Workbook by David Bach
What Should I Do With My Life? by Po Bronson
The Secret by Rhonda Byrne
Key to Living the Law of Attraction by Jack Canfield
Dare to Win by Jack Canfield and Mark Victor Hansen
Michael S. Clouse Blog at http://www.mscmlm.com/
Notes From the Universe at *http://www.tut.com* by Mike Dooley
Left-handed Soldiers by Gary Eby
The Prosperity Bible, The Greatest Writings of All Time on the Secrets to Wealth and Prosperity. Compiled by Jeremy Tarcher
The One Minute Millionaire by Mark Victor Hansen and Robert G. Allen
You Can Heal Your Life by Louise L. Hay
http://www.dreammanifesto.com/ by Thomas Herold
Think and Grow Rich by Napoleon Hill
http://radicalhealth.com/ by David Favor
First Person by Ray C. Hunt
Out of Darkness into The Light by Gerald Jampolsky, M.D.
Inconceivable by Julia Indichova
The Greatest Salesman in the World by Og Mandino

I Can Make You Thin by Paul McKenna
Click! By Annabel Monaghan and Elisabeth Wolfe
Infinite Power for Richer Living by Joseph Murphy
The Power of Your Subconscious Mind by Joseph Murphy
Agents of Change by Kurt-Edouard Neubauer
The Wisdom of Menopause by Christiane Northrup
Become a Better You by Joel Osteen
I'm Rich Beyond My Wildest Dreams by Thomas L. Pauley
        and Penelope J. Pauley
90 Minutes in Heaven by Don Piper
Pulling Weeds to Picking Stocks by the Beatty Boys
Grow Rich While You Sleep by Ben Sweetland
The Message by NavPress Publishing Group
The Power of Now and *A New Earth* by Eckhart Tolle
Making Your Dreams Come True by Marcia Wieder
See You at the Top by Zig Ziglar
SUCCESS Magazine. Stuart Johnson, President and CEO of SUC-
        CESS Media

Bibliography

Bach, David. *The Finish Rich Workbook*. New York: Broadway Books, a division of Random House, Inc., 2003.

Bridgette Bartlett. *I Designed My Dream Wedding on a Dime. http://www.essence.com/relationships/advice/articles/budgetbride*

Bronson, Po. *What Should I Do With My Life?* New York: Random House, 2002.

Buzzle.com, Intelligent Life on the Web. *http://www.buzzle.com/chapters/hobbies-and-special-interest.asp*

Byrne, Rhonda. *The Secret*. New York: Atria Books/Beyond Words Publishing, Inc. 2006.

Canfield, Jack. *Key to Living the Law of Attraction*. Deerfield Beach, FL: Health Communications, Inc., 2007.

Canfield, Jack and Hansen, Mark Victor. *Dare to Win*. New York: Berkley Publishing Group, 1994.

Clouse, Michael S. *Michael S. Clouse Blog. http://www.mscmlm.com/*

Eby, Gary. International Trainer and Sales Strategist. *http://www.garyeby.com*

Haanel, Charles F. "The Master Key System" from *The Prosperity Bible,* The Greatest Writings of All Time on the Secrets to Wealth and Prosperity compiled by Tarcher, Jeremy. Canada: Penguin Group, 2007.

Hansen, Mark Victor and Allen, Robert G. *The One Minute Millionaire*. New York: Harmony Books, 2002.

Hay, Louise L. *You Can Heal Your Life*. Santa Monica, Ca: Hay House, 1984.

Herold, Thomas. http://www.dreammanifesto.com/about-us

Hill, Napoleon. *Think and Grow Rich*. New York: Random House, 1960.

Holtby, Winifred. *O Magazine*, from Laura Moncur's Motivational Quotations, September 2002

Holy Bible, New International Version. International Bible Society, Zondervan, 1973.

Jampolsky, Gerald G. Out of Darkness into The Light. New York: Bantam Books, 1989.

Indichova, Julia. Inconceivable. New York: Broadway Books, 1997.

Leiba, Elizabeth. *http://www.ehow.com/how_2196699_dream-book.html*

LaLanne, Jack. *http://www.jacklalanne.com/*

Lewis, Randine, Ph.D. *The Infertility Cure*. New York: Little, Brown and Company, (Hachette Book Group USA) 2004.

Lorenza, Edward. "Butterfly Effect." A paper for the New York Academy of Sciences noting that *One meteorologist remarked that if the theory were correct, one flap of a butterfly's wings could change the course of weather forever*, 1963.

Mandino, Og. *The Greatest Salesman in the World*. Hollywood, Florida: Frederick Fell Publishing, 1972.

Matthews, Gail. *Goals Research Summary*. *http://www.dominican.edu/academics/artssciences/natbehealth/psych/faculty/gailmatthews.html*. November 2008.

McKenna, Paul. *I Can Make You Thin*. New York: Sterling Publishing Co., Inc., 2009.

Mizrahi, Isaac. *How to Have Style*. New York: Gotham Book published by Penguin Group (USA) Inc., 2008.

Moncur, Laura. http://www.quotationspage.com/mqotd/archive.html. Laura Moncur's Motivational Quotations. *O Magazine*, September 2002.

Murphy, Joseph. *Infinite Power for Richer Living*. New York: Parker Publishing Company, 1969.

Murphy, Joseph. *The Power of Your Subconscious Mind*. New York: Reward Books, 2000.

Neubauer, Kurt-Edouard. *Agents of Change*. United States of America: Xulon Press, 2004.

Northrup, Christiane. *The Wisdom of Menopause*. New York: Bantam Dell, 2001.

Osteen, Joel. *Become a Better You*. New York: Free Press, a division of Simon and Schuster, 2007.

Pauley, Thomas L., and Pauley, Penelope J. *I'm Rich Beyond My Wildest Dreams*. New York: Berkley Publishing Group, 1999.

Piper, Don. *90 Minutes in Heaven*. Fleming H. Revell, a division of Baker Publishing Group: Grand Rapids, MI, 2004.

Sweetland, Ben. *Grow Rich While You Sleep*. New York: Niche Enterprises, LLC, 1978.

The Message. NavPress Publishing Group, 1993.

Tolle, Eckhart. *The Power of Now*. San Rafael, Calif.: New World Library, 1999.

Tolle, Eckhart. *A New Earth*. New York: Plume, a member of Penguin Group, 2005.

Waitley, Denis. *http://www.waitley.com/*

Wattles, Wallace D. "The Science of Getting Rich" from The Prosperity Bible. The Greatest Writings of All Time on the Secrets to Wealth and Prosperity compiled by Tarcher, Jeremy. Canada: Penguin Group, 2007.

Wieder, Marcia. *Making Your Dreams Come True*. New York: Harmony Books, 1999.

Ziglar, Zig. *See You at the Top*. Gretna, LA: Pelican Publishing Company Inc. 1974.